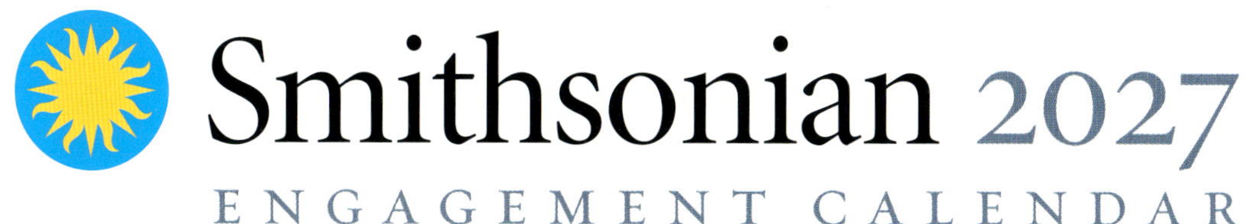
Smithsonian 2027
ENGAGEMENT CALENDAR

AF580221

Published by Smithsonian Books
PO Box 37012, MRC 513
Washington, DC 20013
smithsonianbooks.com

Senior Editor: Jaime Schwender
Editor: Julie Huggins
Copyedited by Tom Fredrickson
Designed by Robert L. Wiser

This calendar may be purchased for educational, business, or sales promotional use. For information please write the Special Markets Department at the address or website above.

Printed in China, not at government expense

A special thanks to Jorge Aleman, Kimberly Arcand, Lisa Austin, Heidi Austreng, Erin Beasley, Julie Botnick, Wesley Chenault, Logan Clark, Rhys Conlon, Ren Cooper, David Coronado, Linda Currie, Miriam Doutriaux, Laura Duff, Linette Dutari, Sarah Elston, Marshall Emery, Angela Ferragamo, Ben Gillespie, Cory Grace, Laura Harger, Paula Healy, Sarah Hedean, Elisa Hough, Janice Hussain, Amy Hutchins, Betsy Johnson, Beth King, Lauren Kolodkin, Fernanda Luppani, Jennifer Mitchell, Robin Morey, Julia Murphy, Timothy Nolan, Cecilia Peterson, Kristen Quarles, Douglas Remley, Marguerite Roby, Jennifer Schneider, Jennifer Schommer, Marie Sicola, Tellie Simpson, Marc Sklar, Kira Sobers, Riche Sorensen, Haley Steinhilber, Amy Strickland, Tanya Thrasher, Kayleigh Walters, Megan Watzke, Kelly Williamson, and Jennifer Zoon.

Photographs are of objects in the collections of the museums and research facilities that make up the Smithsonian. Special thanks to Smithsonian photographers Ernest Amoroso, Mark Avino, Rick Coulby, James Di Loreto, Matt Flynn, Katherine Fogden (Mohawk), Mark Gulezian, Brittany M. Hance, Andrew Innerarity, Alex Jamison, John Franko Khoury, Victor Krantz, Hannele Lahti, Phillip R. Lee, Lucia RM Martino, Jaclyn Nash, Roshan Patel, Steve Paton, Sonya Pencheva, Jessica Scott, and Brad Simpson.

Equinox, solstice, and moon phase dates are given according to Eastern Standard Time or Eastern Daylight Saving Time as applicable.

● New Moon ◐ First Quarter ○ Full Moon ◑ Last Quarter

For previsit planning material, please contact: Smithsonian Information, Smithsonian Institution, SI Building, Room 153, PO Box 37012, MRC 010, Washington, DC 20013-7012, 202-633-1000 (voice). Send email inquiries to info@si.edu. Visit us on the web at www.si.edu/visit.

To order Smithsonian engagement calendars: Please visit www.smithsonianstore.com or call 1-800-322-0344. Shipping and handling charges will apply.

Front Cover:
Hwajodo, late 19th century
Korea, Joseon period
Glue, ink, paper
36¼ × 20½ in.
(92 × 52 cm)
National Museum
of Natural History

This *hwajodo*—or bird-and-flower painting—features pheasants, swallows, and plum blossoms, capturing the nature and fertility themes common in *minhwa*, or Korean folk art from the Joseon period (1392–1910). *Hwajodo* were typically painted on folding screens and depicted pairs of animals to symbolize a happy marriage; thus, they were often used to decorate newlyweds' bedrooms.

The Lissochilus-like Vanda
(*Vandopsis lissochiloides*)
Digital photograph by
Hannele Lahti, August 2024
Washington, DC
Smithsonian Gardens

Vandopsis lissochiloides is a giant, jungle-growing orchid that can have flower spikes up to eight feet tall. It grows natively from mainland Southeast Asia to Western New Guinea and is one of only two members of its genus. The flowers of the Lissochilus-like Vanda are long lasting and sweet scented.

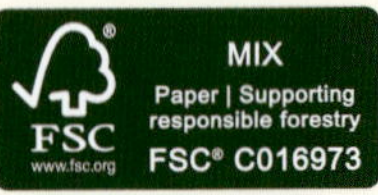

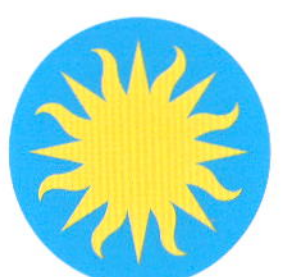

Smithsonian 2027

ENGAGEMENT CALENDAR

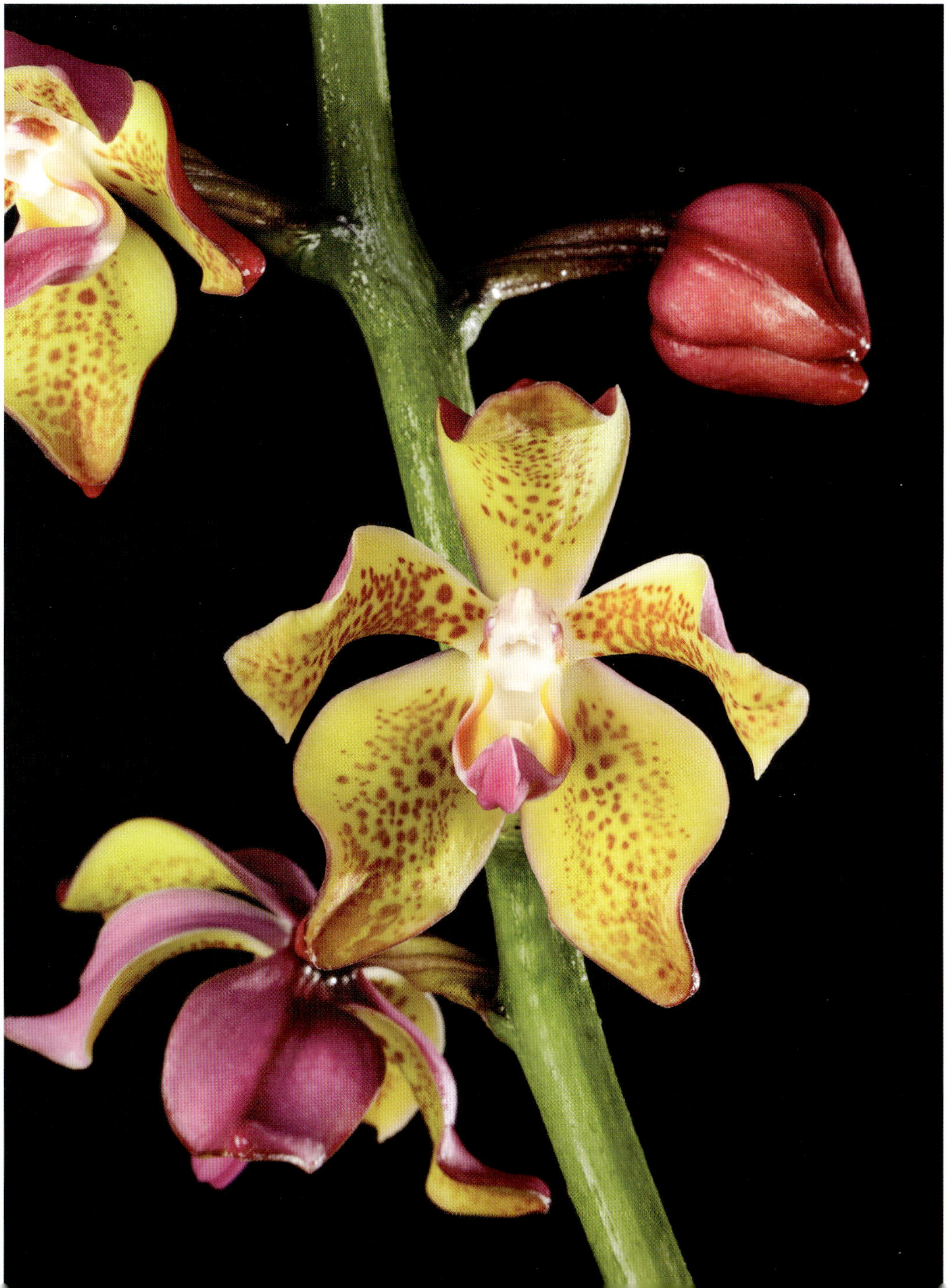

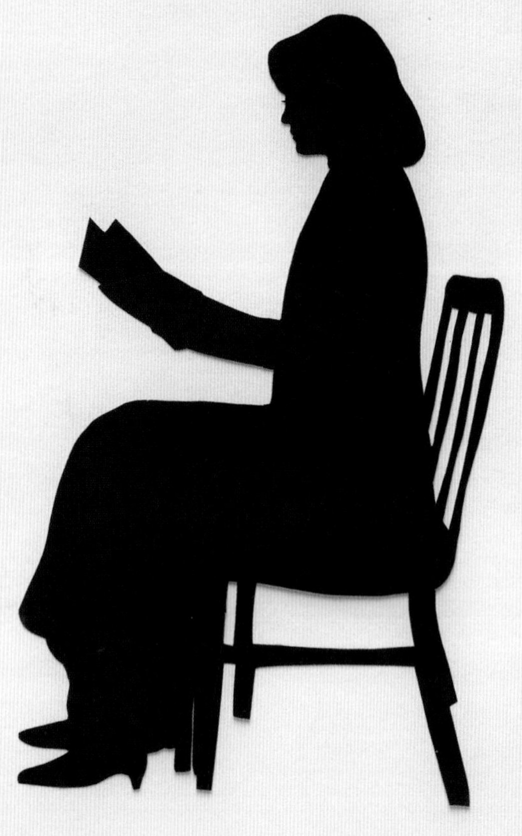

DECEMBER · JANUARY

Helen Laughon (1919–2018) and Nel Laughon (1946–2011)
Diane Sawyer, 1987
Cut-paper silhouette
14 × 11⅛ in.
(35.6 × 28.3 cm)
Gift of the family of Helen and Nel Laughon
National Portrait Gallery

After beginning her career as a press aide in Richard Nixon's White House, Diane Sawyer (b. 1945) went on to become the first woman to co-anchor CBS's primetime news program *60 Minutes* (1984–89). She later anchored several flagship programs on ABC, including *Good Morning America* (1999–2009) and *ABC World News Tonight* (2009–14).

SUNDAY
27

MONDAY
28

TUESDAY
29

◑
WEDNESDAY
30

NEW YEAR'S EVE
THURSDAY
31

NEW YEAR'S DAY · KWANZAA ENDS
FRIDAY
1

SATURDAY
2

DECEMBER 2026

S	M	T	W	T	F	S
		1	2	3	4	5
6	7	8	9	10	11	12
13	14	15	16	17	18	19
20	21	22	23	24	25	26
27	28	29	30	31		

JANUARY

S	M	T	W	T	F	S
					1	2
3	4	5	6	7	8	9
10	11	12	13	14	15	16
17	18	19	20	21	22	23
24	25	26	27	28	29	30
31						

JANUARY

SUNDAY

3

MONDAY

4

TUESDAY

5

WEDNESDAY

6

THURSDAY

7 ●

FRIDAY

8

SATURDAY

9

Jontay Kahm
(Plains Cree, b. 1996)
Bell Bird, 2022
Felt, satin, goose feathers, glue
42½ × 35½ × 23½ in.
(108 × 90 × 60 cm)
National Museum of the American Indian

The designer Jontay Kahm titled this dress after the world's loudest bird: the male white bellbird. Its call sounds like a bell and can reach up to 125 decibels, equivalent to the sound produced by a jackhammer. To give the appearance of being engulfed by sound, Kahm attached 800 dyed goose feathers in undulating waves around the shoulders and waist of the garment.

JANUARY

S	M	T	W	T	F	S
					1	2
3	4	5	6	7	8	9
10	11	12	13	14	15	16
17	18	19	20	21	22	23
24	25	26	27	28	29	30
31						

FEBRUARY

S	M	T	W	T	F	S
	1	2	3	4	5	6
7	8	9	10	11	12	13
14	15	16	17	18	19	20
21	22	23	24	25	26	27
28						

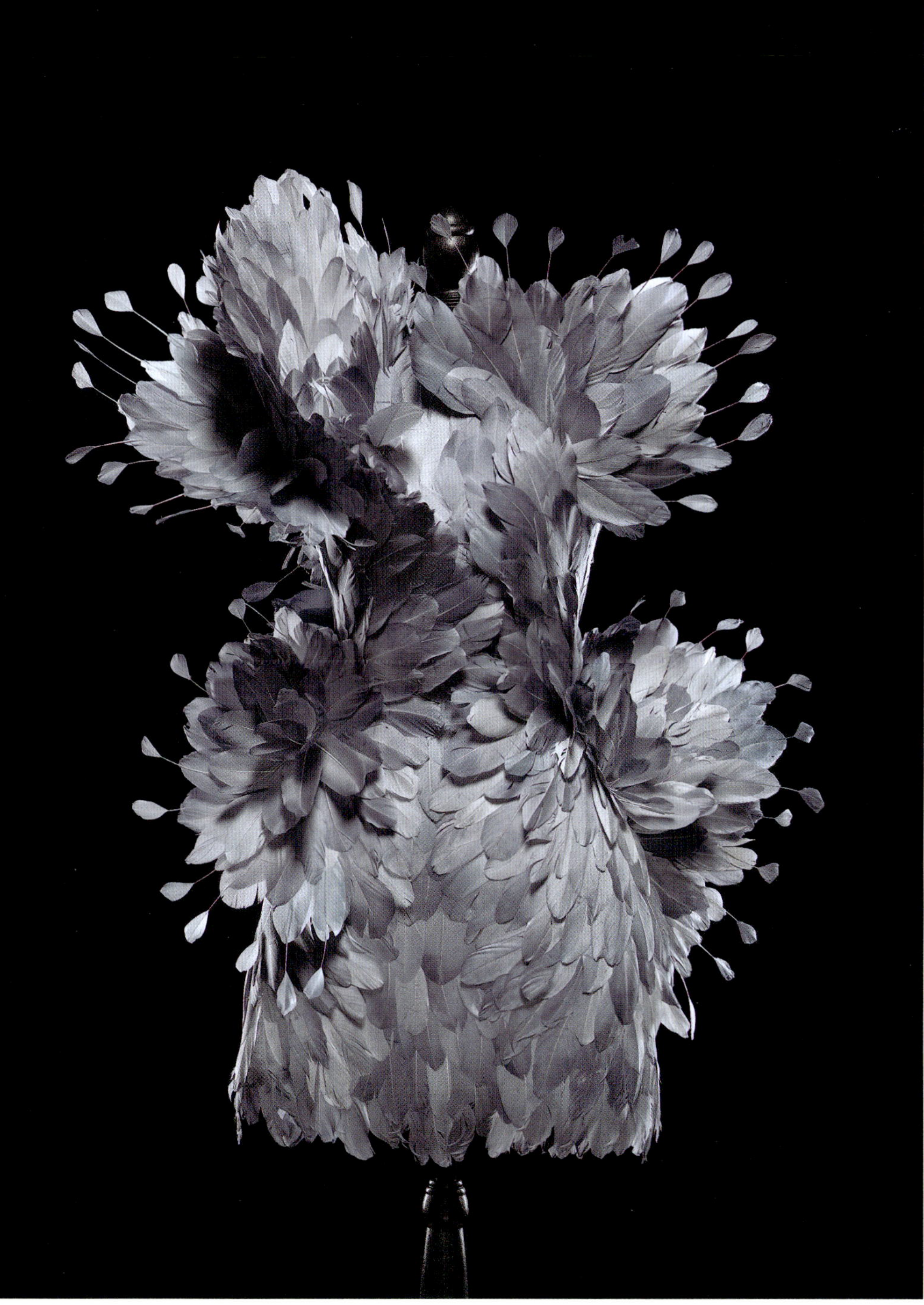

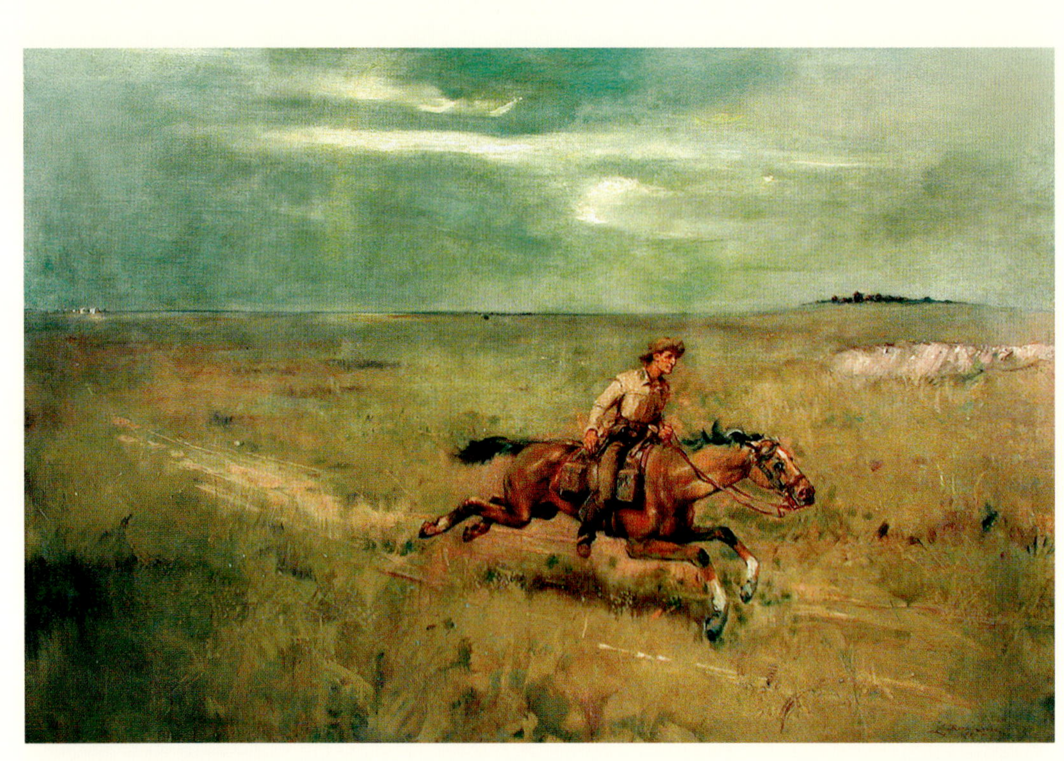

JANUARY

Attributed to Lloyd Branson (1853–1925)
Pony Express Rider, 1904
Oil on canvas
62¼ × 93 in.
(158 × 236 cm)
National Postal Museum

In 1860 William Russell, Alexander Majors, and William Bradford Waddell founded the Pony Express, a privately owned mail-delivery service that used horse-mounted riders to deliver mail across the American West. Riders could be identified by special bags—*mochilas*—that were designed to fit over a saddle and carry mail.

SUNDAY
10

MONDAY
11

TUESDAY
12

WEDNESDAY
13

THURSDAY
14

◐

FRIDAY
15

SATURDAY
16

JANUARY

S	M	T	W	T	F	S
					1	2
3	4	5	6	7	8	9
10	11	12	13	14	15	16
17	18	19	20	21	22	23
24	25	26	27	28	29	30
31						

FEBRUARY

S	M	T	W	T	F	S
	1	2	3	4	5	6
7	8	9	10	11	12	13
14	15	16	17	18	19	20
21	22	23	24	25	26	27
28						

JANUARY

SUNDAY

17

MONDAY MARTIN LUTHER KING JR. DAY

18

TUESDAY

19

WEDNESDAY

20

THURSDAY

21

FRIDAY ○

22

SATURDAY

23

Banjo played by
Lew Snowden, 1870s
Nickel, wood,
animal skin, ivory
33½ × 12 × 3½ in.
(85 × 30.5 × 9 cm)
Gift of Howard L. Sacks and Judith Rose Sacks from the Snowden Collection
National Museum of American History

Lew Snowden was a member of the Snowden Family Band, an ensemble of Black farmers who performed across rural Ohio from the 1850s to the early 1920s. This banjo, engraved LD SNOWDEN, represented the hard-fought freedom Snowden and his siblings found in travel, song, and music-making.

JANUARY

S	M	T	W	T	F	S
					1	2
3	4	5	6	7	8	9
10	11	12	13	14	15	16
17	18	19	20	21	22	23
24	25	26	27	28	29	30
31						

FEBRUARY

S	M	T	W	T	F	S
	1	2	3	4	5	6
7	8	9	10	11	12	13
14	15	16	17	18	19	20
21	22	23	24	25	26	27
28						

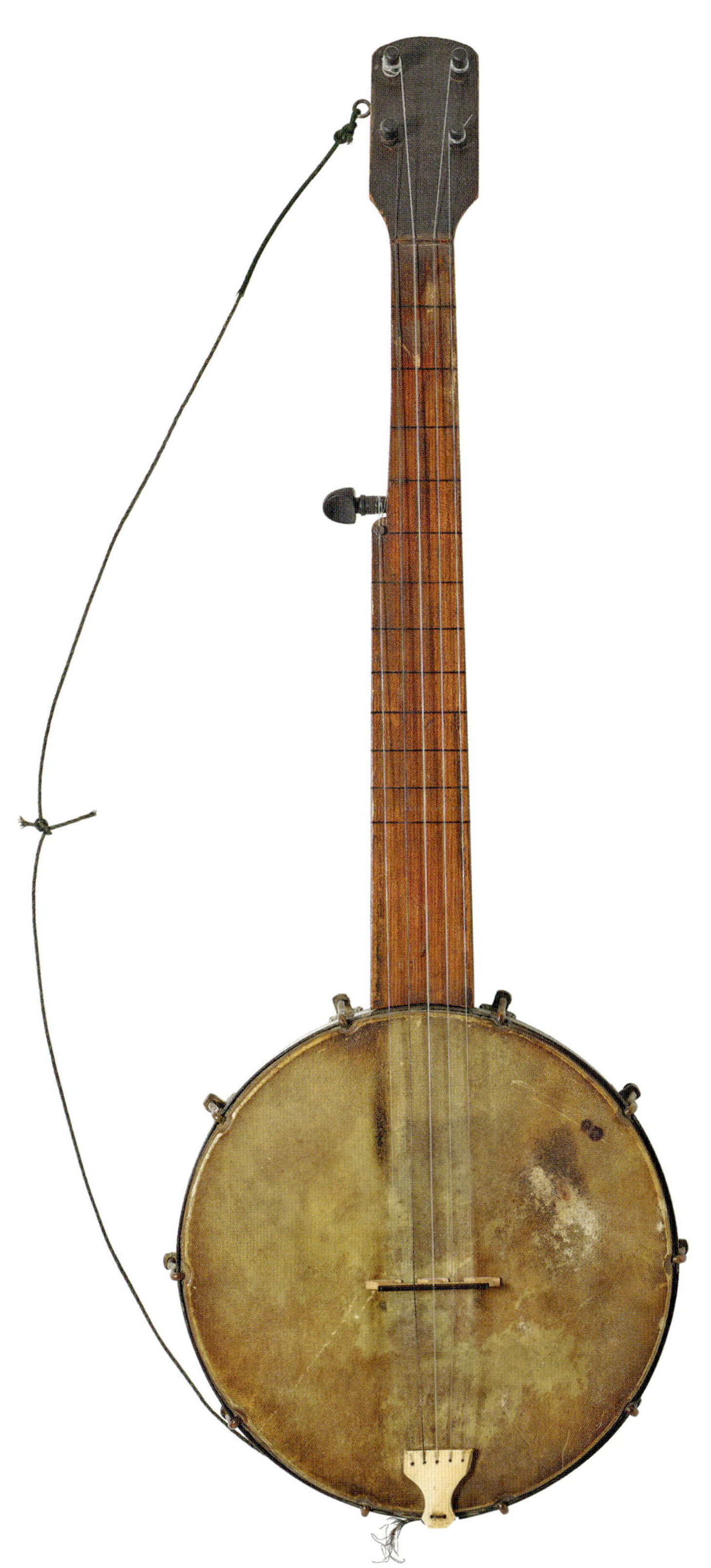

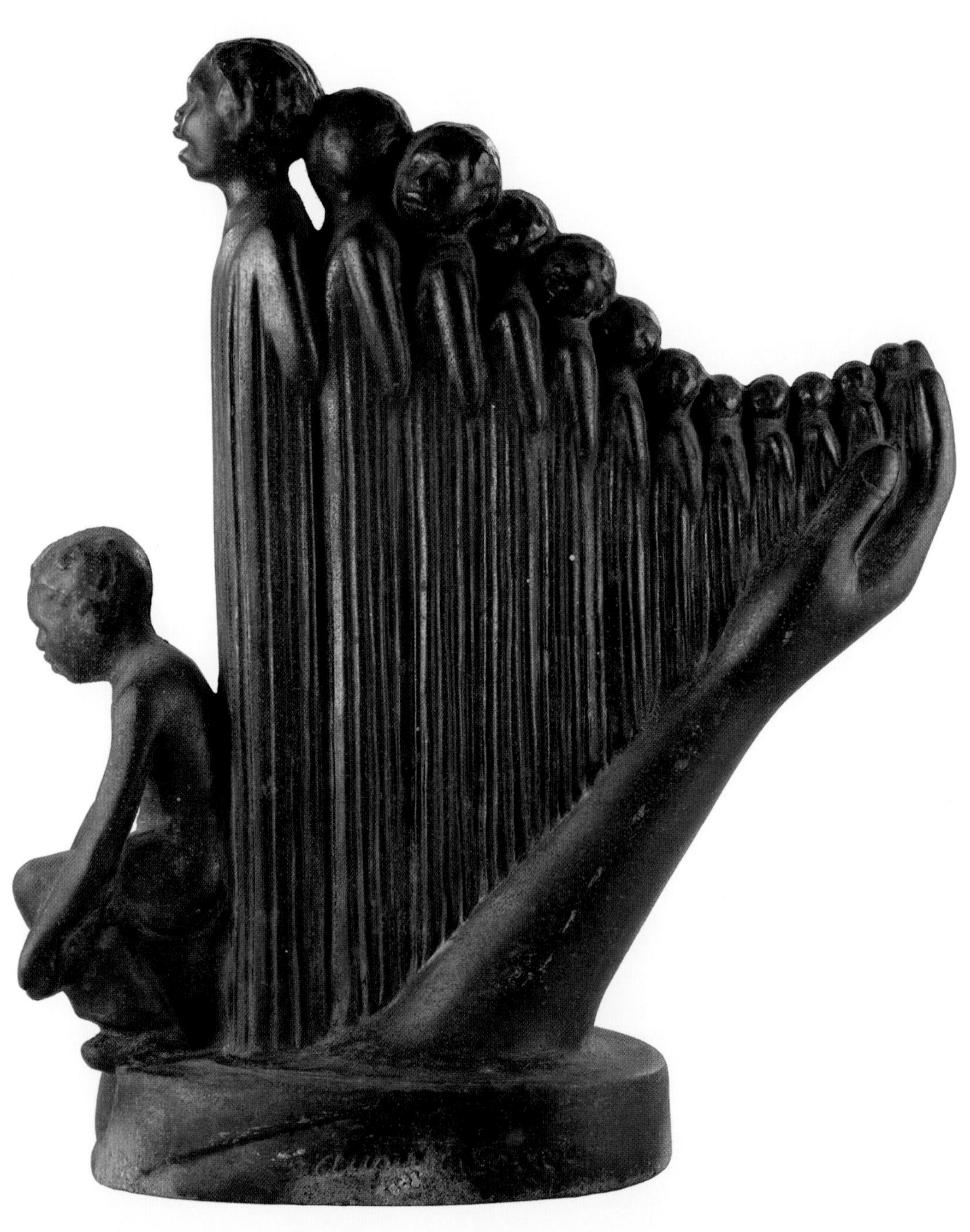

JANUARY

Augusta Savage (1892–1962)
Lift Every Voice and Sing (The Harp), c. 1939
Metal
10 13/16 × 4 × 10½ in.
(27.5 × 10.2 × 26 cm)
Gift of the Blount, Holloway, and Edgerton Families
National Museum of African American History and Culture

A key figure in the Harlem Renaissance, the sculptor and educator Augusta Savage was commissioned to create a work celebrating African American music for the 1939 New York World's Fair. The result was a sixteen-foot-tall plaster sculpture titled *Lift Every Voice and Sing*, inspired by James Weldon Johnson's poem and song of the same name. When the original was destroyed at the fair's end, Savage produced smaller souvenir replicas like this one.

SUNDAY
24

MONDAY
25

TUESDAY
26

WEDNESDAY
27

THURSDAY
28

◑

FRIDAY
29

SATURDAY
30

JANUARY

S	M	T	W	T	F	S
					1	2
3	4	5	6	7	8	9
10	11	12	13	14	15	16
17	18	19	20	21	22	23
24	25	26	27	28	29	30
31						

FEBRUARY

S	M	T	W	T	F	S
	1	2	3	4	5	6
7	8	9	10	11	12	13
14	15	16	17	18	19	20
21	22	23	24	25	26	27
28						

JANUARY · FEBRUARY

SUNDAY

31

MONDAY

1

TUESDAY

2

WEDNESDAY

3

THURSDAY

4

FRIDAY

5

SATURDAY

LUNAR NEW YEAR ●

6

Rank badge (*hyungbae*), late 19th century
Korea, Joseon period
Silk, gilded paper, embroidery on silk damask
9¾ × 8½ in. (25 × 21.5 cm)
Gift of the estate of Mrs. Lathrop Colgate Harper
Cooper Hewitt, Smithsonian Design Museum

Korea's Joseon dynasty (1392–1910) employed badges embroidered with animals to distinguish the ranks of its officials. This badge has two vividly expressive leopards surrounded by cloud motifs, coral branches, rocks, and water. Standards set in 1871 dictated that badges featuring two leopards were reserved for senior military officers.

JANUARY

S	M	T	W	T	F	S
					1	2
3	4	5	6	7	8	9
10	11	12	13	14	15	16
17	18	19	20	21	22	23
24	25	26	27	28	29	30
31						

FEBRUARY

S	M	T	W	T	F	S
	1	2	3	4	5	6
7	8	9	10	11	12	13
14	15	16	17	18	19	20
21	22	23	24	25	26	27
28						

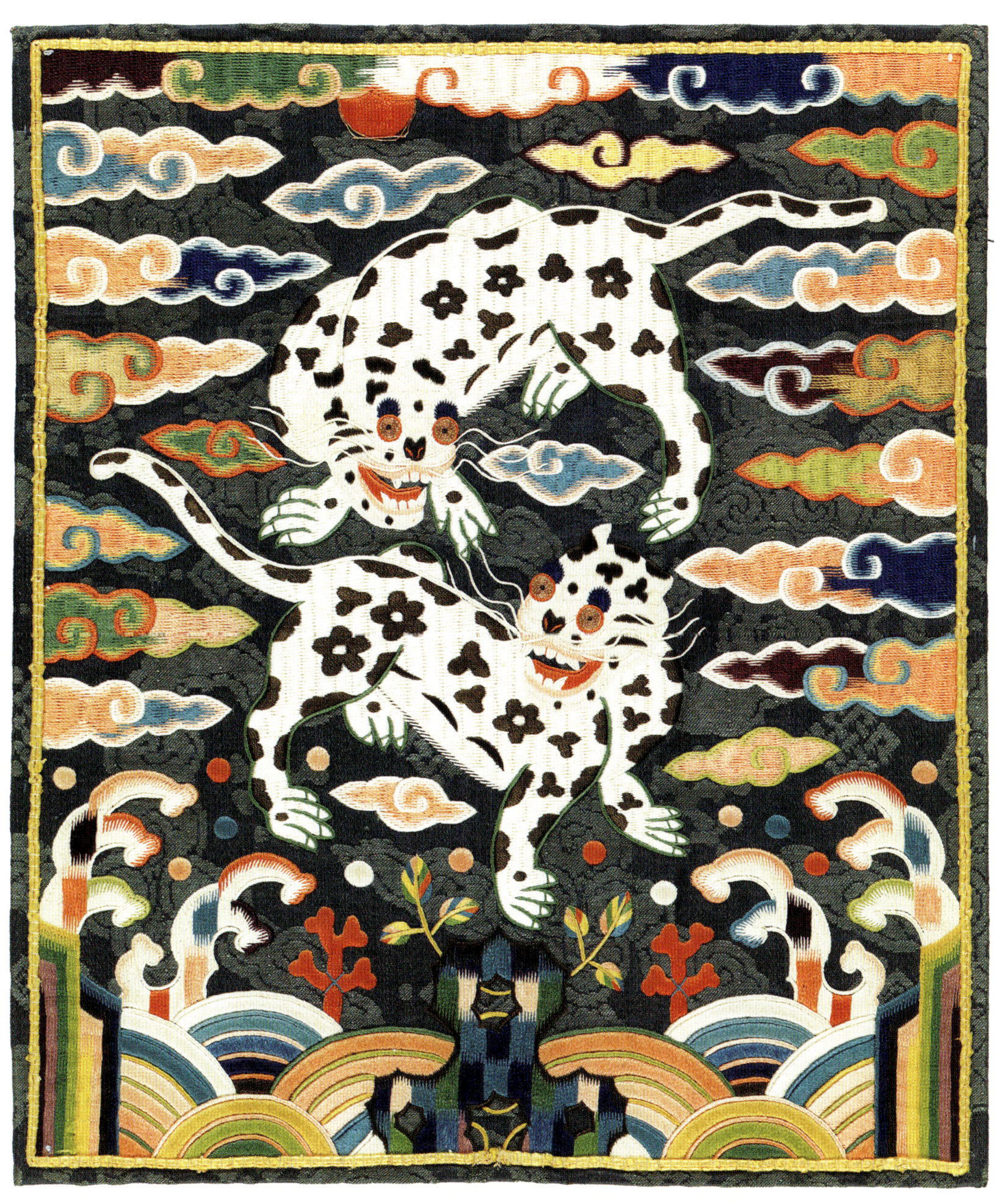

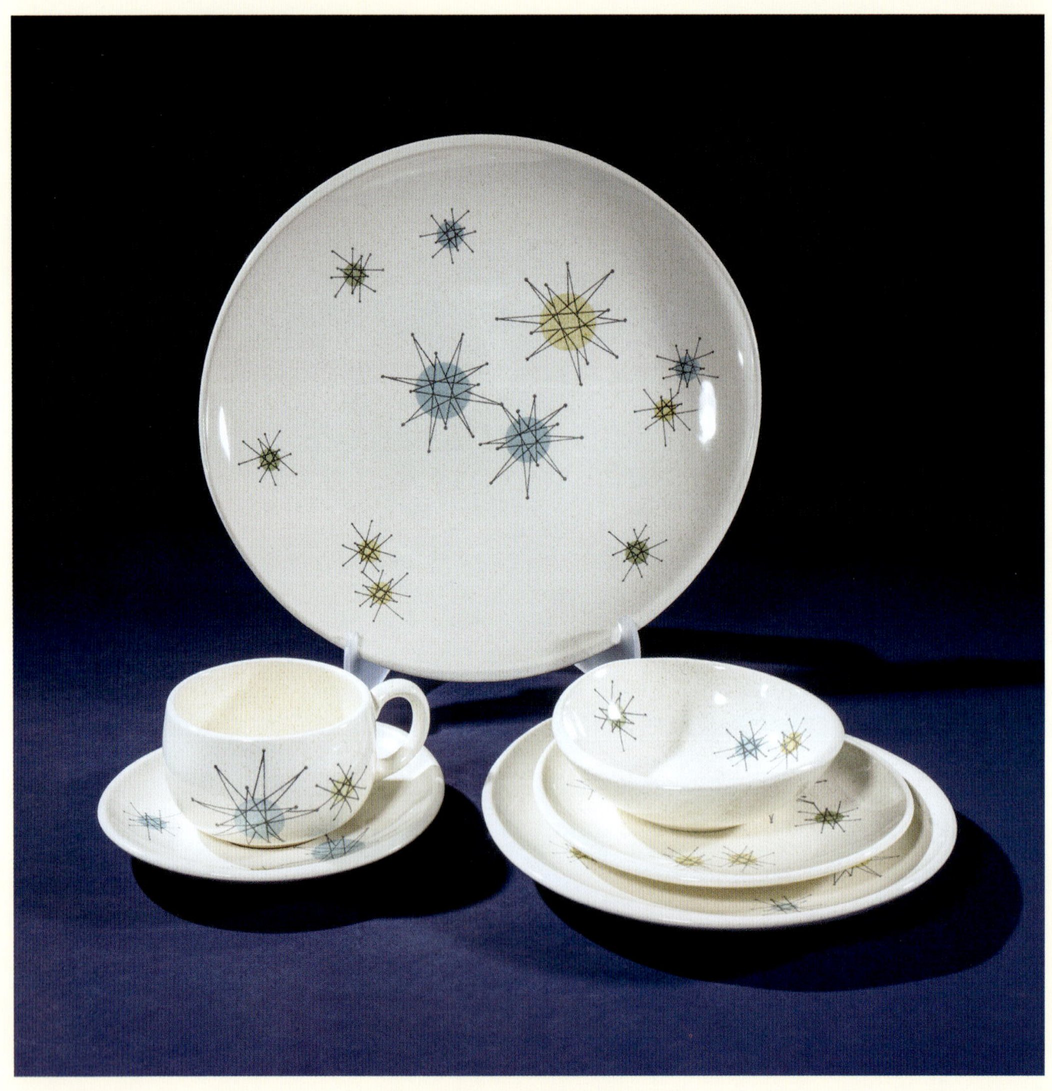

FEBRUARY

Starburst pattern
dinnerware, 1953
Franciscan Ceramics,
Los Angeles
Ceramic
Dinner plate diameter:
10⅞ in. (27.6 cm)
National Air
and Space Museum

When this set of dinnerware debuted, space was a new frontier, and the "Starburst" pattern signified that the future was fast approaching. The design features black electron-like dots tracing star-shaped paths around blue, yellow, and olive green nuclei. These pieces, part of the Modern Americana line by Franciscan Ceramics, illustrate how enthusiasm about mid-century transformations found expression in all kinds of consumer products, even dishware.

FEBRUARY

S	M	T	W	T	F	S
	1	2	3	4	5	6
7	8	9	10	11	12	13
14	15	16	17	18	19	20
21	22	23	24	25	26	27
28						

MARCH

S	M	T	W	T	F	S
	1	2	3	4	5	6
7	8	9	10	11	12	13
14	15	16	17	18	19	20
21	22	23	24	25	26	27
28	29	30	31			

RAMADAN BEGINS (SUNDOWN)

SUNDAY

7

MONDAY

8

TUESDAY

9

ASH WEDNESDAY

WEDNESDAY

10

THURSDAY

11

FRIDAY

12

SATURDAY

13

FEBRUARY

SUNDAY — VALENTINE'S DAY ◐

14

MONDAY — PRESIDENTS' DAY

15

TUESDAY

16

WEDNESDAY

17

THURSDAY

18

FRIDAY

19

SATURDAY ○

20

Eliot Elisofon (1911–1973)
Waterfall on the Tshopo River, Kisangani, Congo (Democratic Republic), 1972
35mm color slide
Eliot Elisofon Photographic Archives
National Museum of African Art

This photograph was taken by the famed photojournalist Eliot Elisofon when he was on assignment for *National Geographic*. The Tshopo River, pictured here, produces hydroelectric power that provides electricity to primarily urban areas. The National Museum of African Art's Eliot Elisofon Photographic Archives, a rich trove of Africa's visual history, is named for the photographer.

FEBRUARY

S	M	T	W	T	F	S
	1	2	3	4	5	6
7	8	9	10	11	12	13
14	15	16	17	18	19	20
21	22	23	24	25	26	27
28						

MARCH

S	M	T	W	T	F	S
	1	2	3	4	5	6
7	8	9	10	11	12	13
14	15	16	17	18	19	20
21	22	23	24	25	26	27
28	29	30	31			

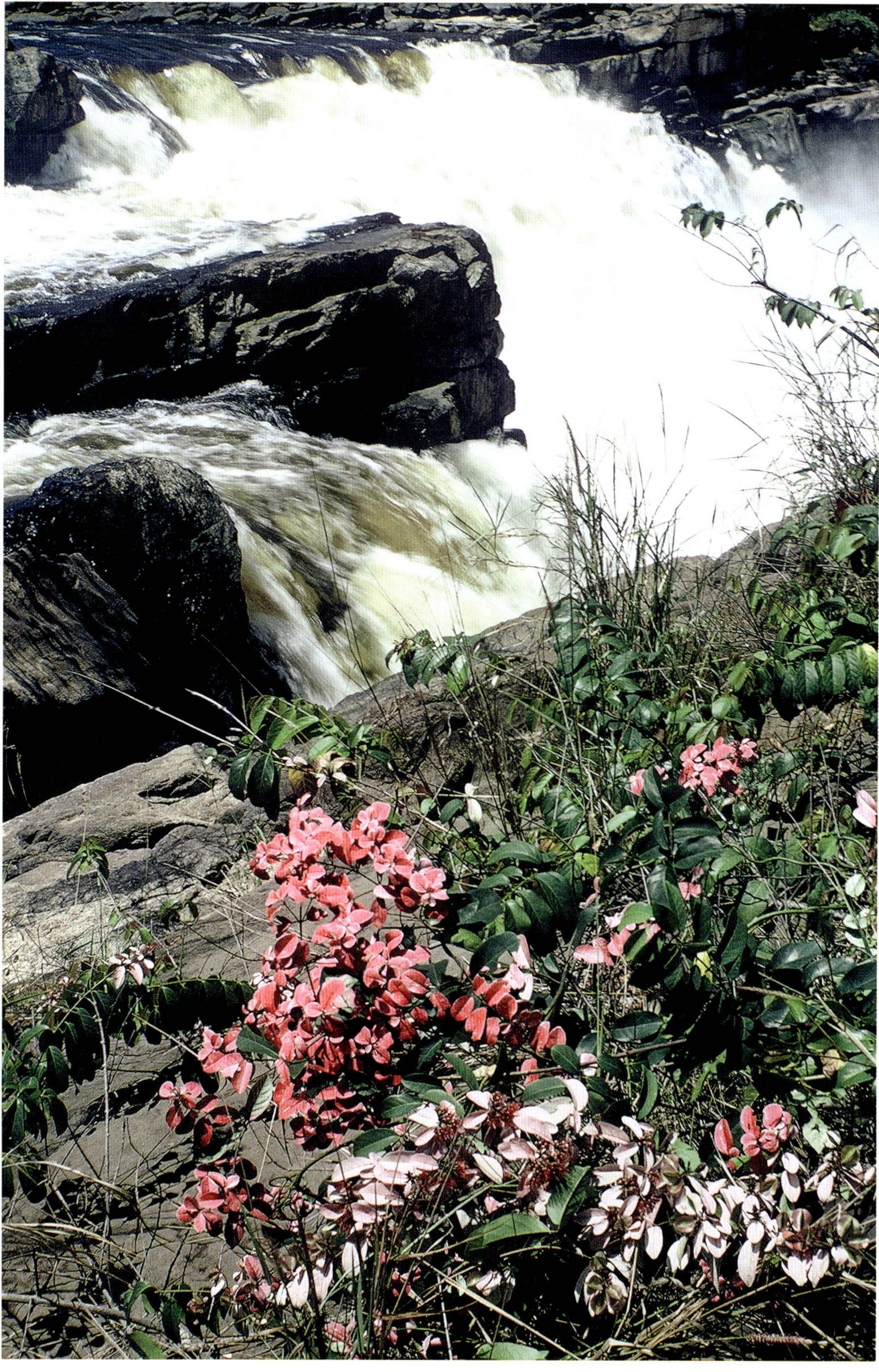

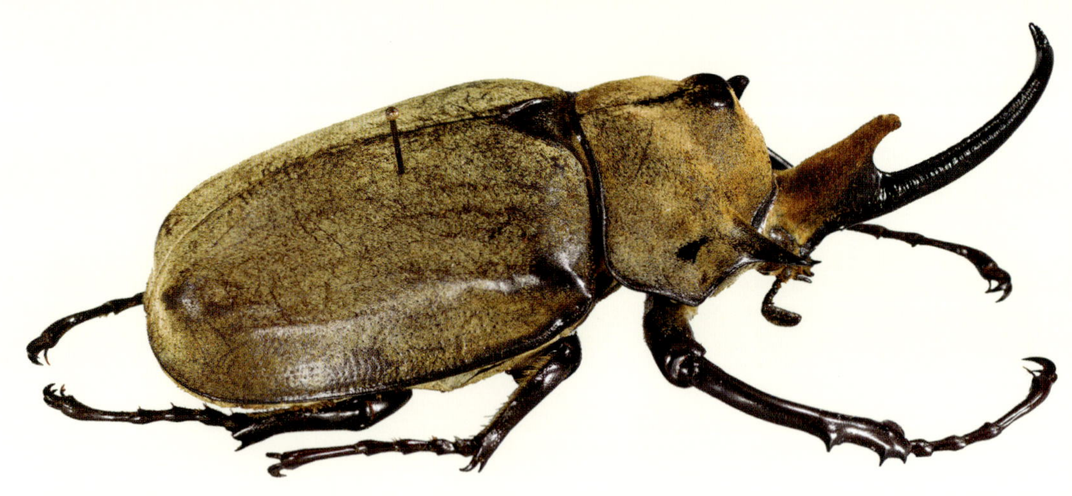

FEBRUARY

Elephant beetle
(*Megasoma elephas elephas*)
Mexico
3 × 4¾ in. (7.6 × 12.1 cm)
National Museum
of Natural History

The elephant beetle, native to the rainforests of North and South America, belongs to a subfamily of scarabs known, ironically enough, as rhinoceros beetles, so called for the males' distinctive horns. Including their curved, trunk-like horns, used for protection and fighting, male elephant beetles have been known to reach lengths of nearly 5½ inches.

FEBRUARY

S	M	T	W	T	F	S
	1	2	3	4	5	6
7	8	9	10	11	12	13
14	15	16	17	18	19	20
21	22	23	24	25	26	27
28						

MARCH

S	M	T	W	T	F	S
	1	2	3	4	5	6
7	8	9	10	11	12	13
14	15	16	17	18	19	20
21	22	23	24	25	26	27
28	29	30	31			

SUNDAY

21

MONDAY

22

TUESDAY

23

WEDNESDAY

24

THURSDAY

25

FRIDAY

26

SATURDAY

27

FEBRUARY · MARCH

SUNDAY ◑

28

MONDAY

1

TUESDAY

2

WEDNESDAY

3

THURSDAY

4

FRIDAY

5

SATURDAY

6

David Driskell (1931–2020)
Night Vision (Homage to Jacob Lawrence), 2007
Screen print, collage on paper
41½ × 28¼ in.
(105.5 × 72 cm)
Anacostia Community Museum

Driskell often used masklike faces in his art to express the power and continuing presence of ancestors. In this luminous celebration of his mentor, Jacob Lawrence, a figure with a bifurcated face emerges from a blue background.

FEBRUARY

S	M	T	W	T	F	S
	1	2	3	4	5	6
7	8	9	10	11	12	13
14	15	16	17	18	19	20
21	22	23	24	25	26	27
28						

MARCH

S	M	T	W	T	F	S
	1	2	3	4	5	6
7	8	9	10	11	12	13
14	15	16	17	18	19	20
21	22	23	24	25	26	27
28	29	30	31			

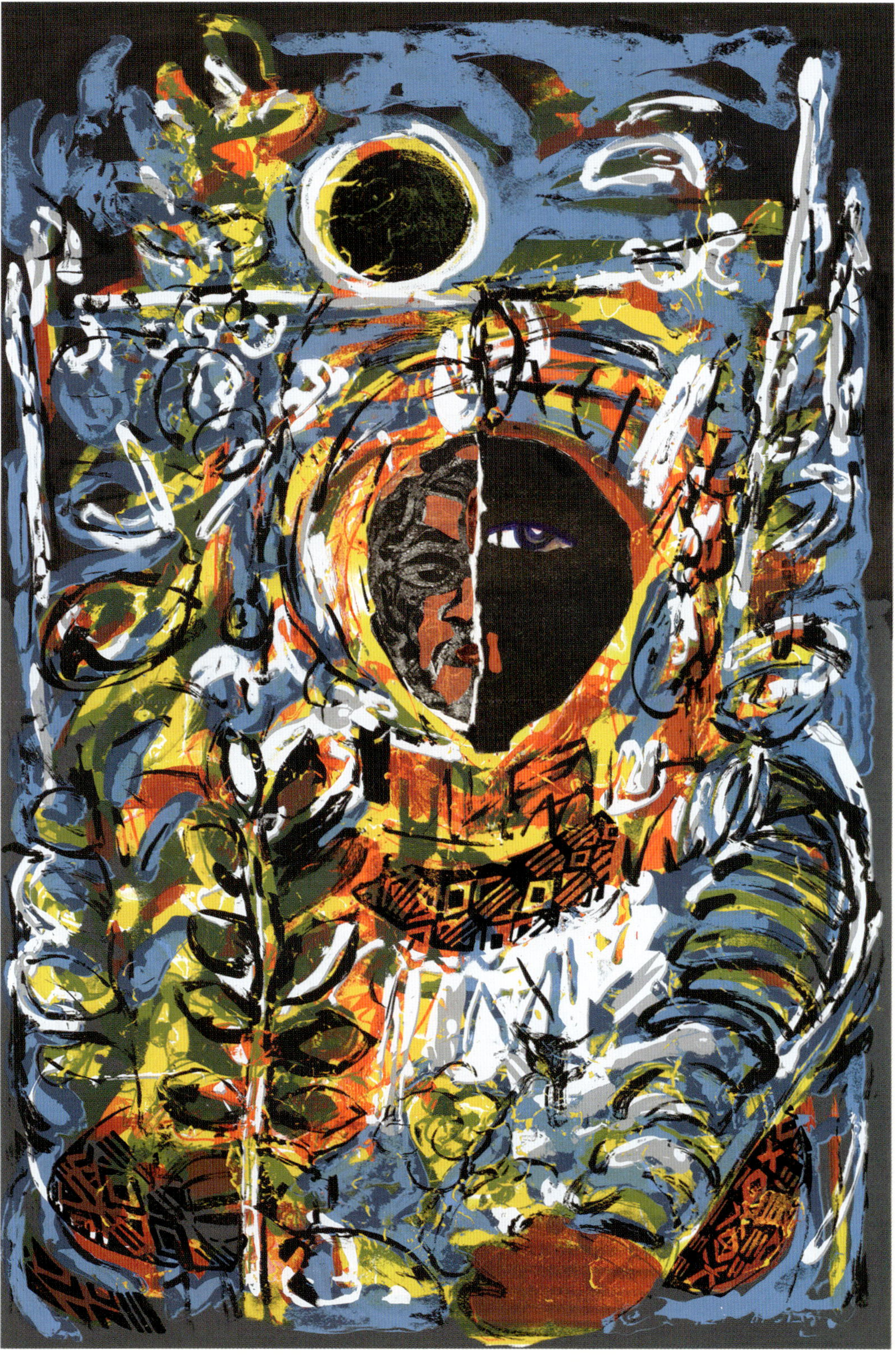

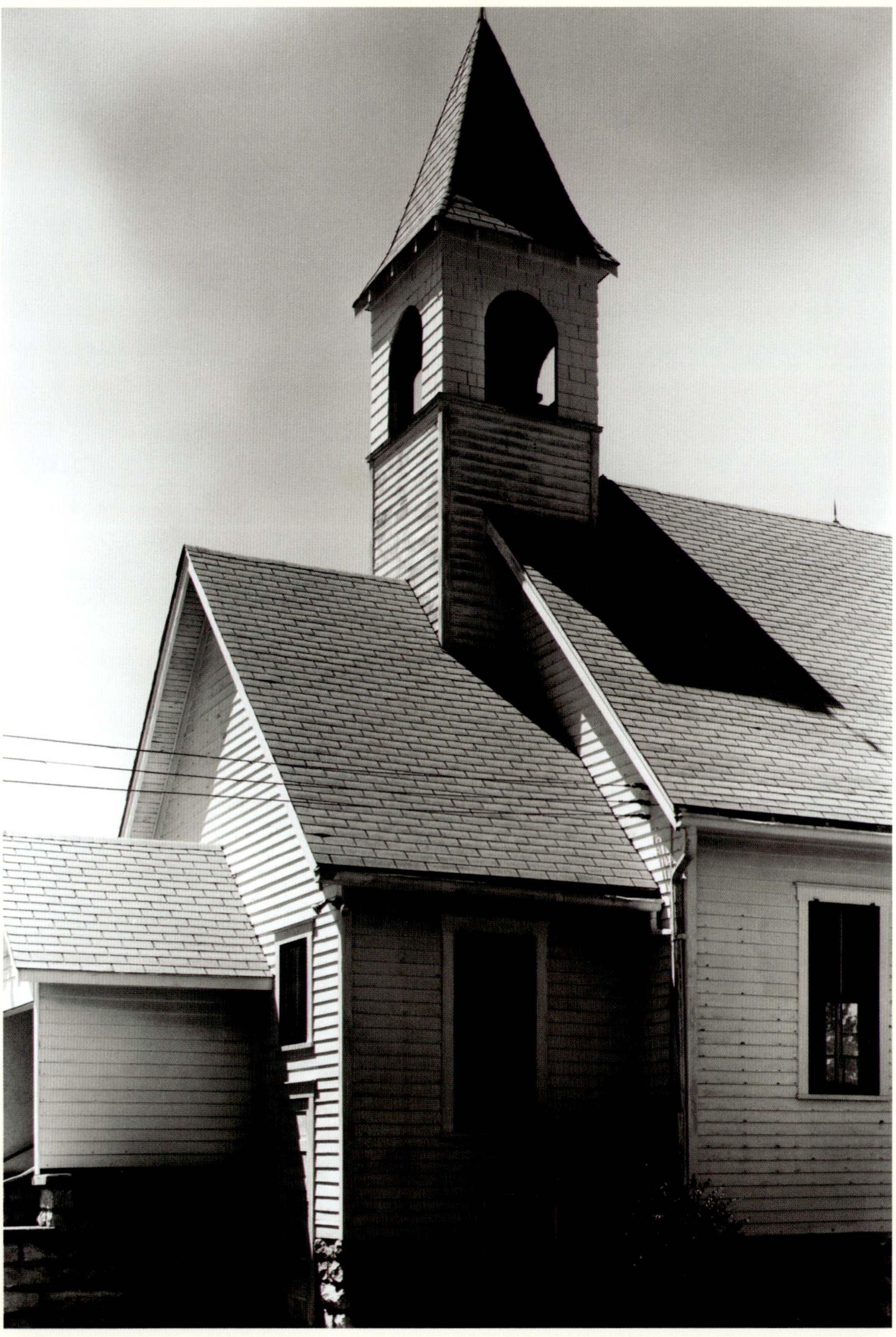

James L. Enyeart (b. 1943)
Vinland, from the
Kansas Documentary
Survey Project, 1974
Gelatin silver print
9⅞ × 7 in.
(25.1 × 17.8 cm)
Smithsonian American
Art Museum

In the 1970s the National Endowment for the Arts sponsored a series of projects inspired by the epic documentary photography program undertaken by the federal government in the 1930s and 1940s. In 1974, photographer and curator James Enyeart, along with Kansas natives Terry Evans and Larry Schwarm, traveled across the state, photographing whatever struck them as representative of the land where there were "no mountains in the way."

MARCH

S	M	T	W	T	F	S
	1	2	3	4	5	6
7	8	9	10	11	12	13
14	15	16	17	18	19	20
21	22	23	24	25	26	27
28	29	30	31			

APRIL

S	M	T	W	T	F	S
				1	2	3
4	5	6	7	8	9	10
11	12	13	14	15	16	17
18	19	20	21	22	23	24
25	26	27	28	29	30	

MARCH

SUNDAY
7

●
MONDAY
8

RAMADAN ENDS (SUNDOWN)
TUESDAY
9

WEDNESDAY
10

THURSDAY
11

FRIDAY
12

SATURDAY
13

MARCH

SUNDAY — DAYLIGHT SAVING TIME BEGINS

14

MONDAY ◐

15

TUESDAY

16

WEDNESDAY — ST. PATRICK'S DAY

17

THURSDAY

18

FRIDAY

19

SATURDAY — FIRST DAY OF SPRING

20

Rufous-collared sparrow
(*Zonotrichia capensis*)
Digital photograph by
Steven Paton, August 2021
Cerro Punta, Panama
Smithsonian Tropical
Research Institute

Rufous-collared sparrows are found in Panama's Chiriqui highlands, where researchers study how birds use coffee plantations to forage for insects and berries and rest in the shade offered by plants, among other activities. This research helps environmentalists better protect these vital parts of our ecosystem.

MARCH

S	M	T	W	T	F	S
	1	2	3	4	5	6
7	8	9	10	11	12	13
14	15	16	17	18	19	20
21	22	23	24	25	26	27
28	29	30	31			

APRIL

S	M	T	W	T	F	S
				1	2	3
4	5	6	7	8	9	10
11	12	13	14	15	16	17
18	19	20	21	22	23	24
25	26	27	28	29	30	

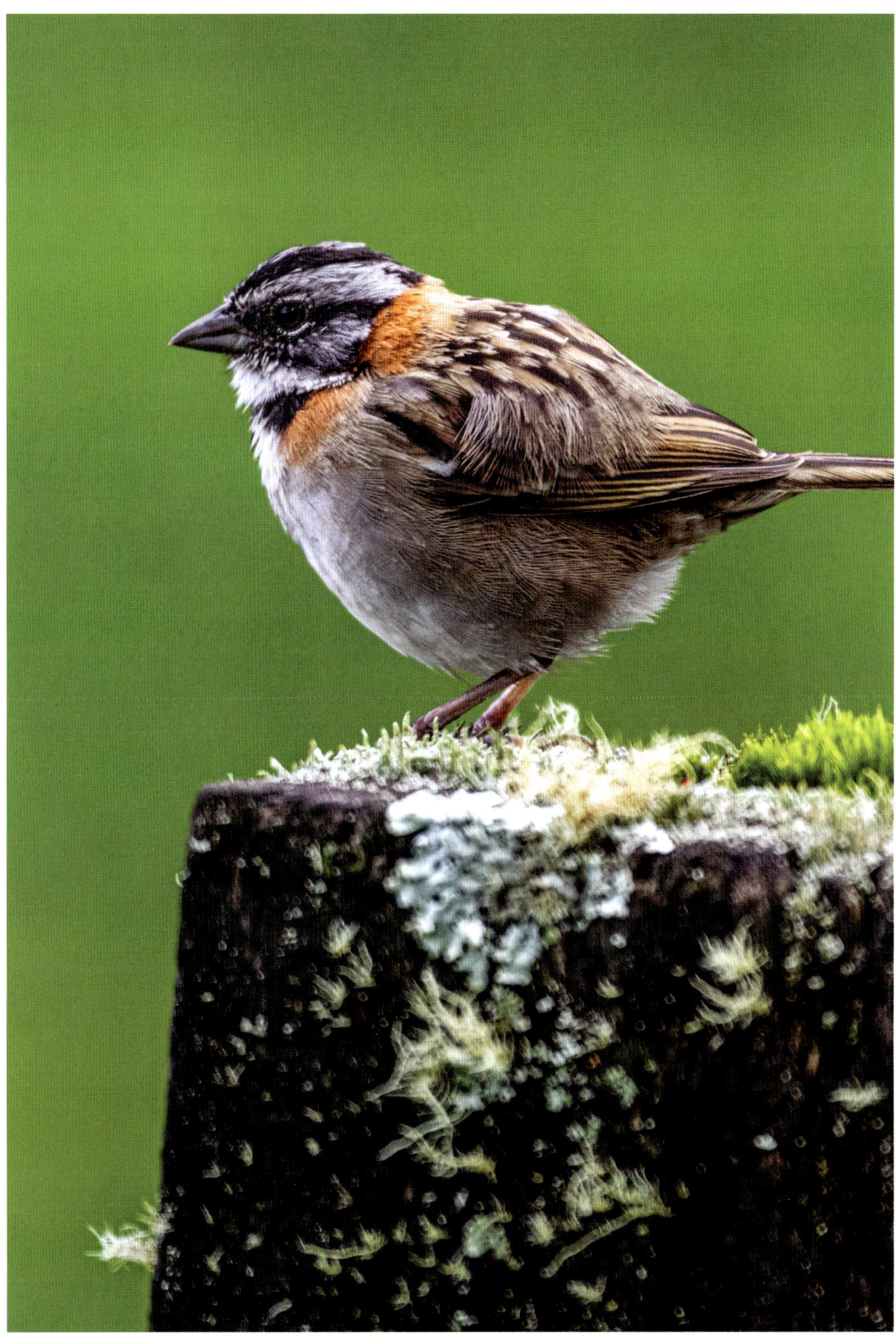

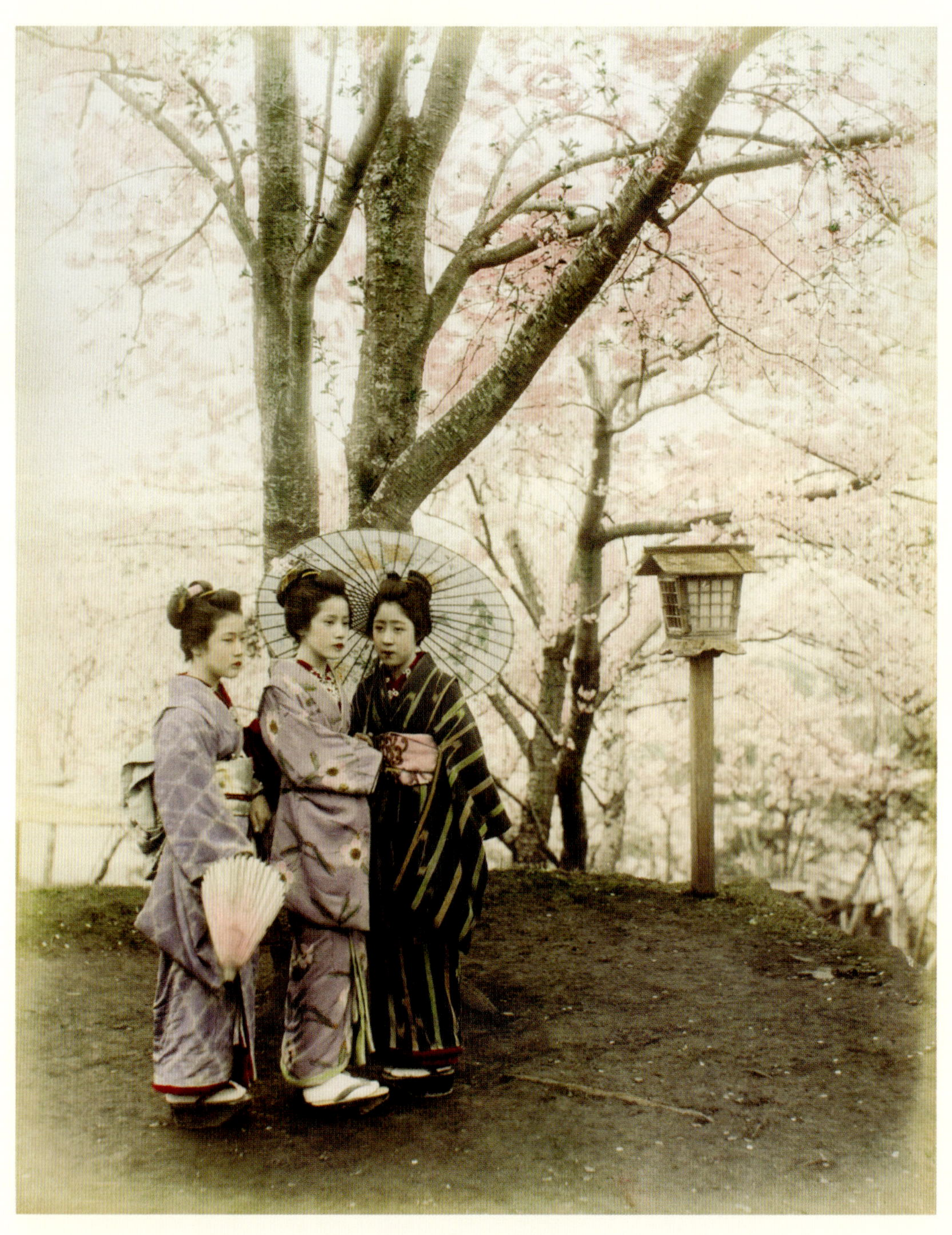

MARCH

Three women with parasols under cherry blossoms, late 19th century
Studio of Tamamura Kozaburo (b. 1856)
Yokohama, Japan
Hand-colored photograph
9¼ x 7½ in.
(24 x 19.2 cm)
National Museum of Asian Art

This image of three women posing beneath a blooming cherry tree captures the beauty of early spring in Japan. It was published for the tourist trade by the studio of Tamamura Kozaburo, who opened a photography shop in 1874 in Asakusa, Tokyo, before moving to Yokohama in 1883.

PALM SUNDAY

SUNDAY
21

○

MONDAY
22

HOLI

TUESDAY
23

WEDNESDAY
24

THURSDAY
25

GOOD FRIDAY

FRIDAY
26

SATURDAY
27

MARCH

S	M	T	W	T	F	S
	1	2	3	4	5	6
7	8	9	10	11	12	13
14	15	16	17	18	19	20
21	22	23	24	25	26	27
28	29	30	31			

APRIL

S	M	T	W	T	F	S
				1	2	3
4	5	6	7	8	9	10
11	12	13	14	15	16	17
18	19	20	21	22	23	24
25	26	27	28	29	30	

MARCH • APRIL

SUNDAY — EASTER

28

MONDAY — EASTER MONDAY (CAN.) ◑

29

TUESDAY

30

WEDNESDAY

31

THURSDAY

1

FRIDAY

2

SATURDAY

3

A field of blooming tulips in the Netherlands
Digital photograph by user IIIIESPDJ, iStock
Kinderdijk, Netherlands
Smithsonian Journeys

The sun rises over two symbols of the Netherlands—tulips and windmills—whose stories are intertwined. Beginning in the 1400s, the Dutch built polder windmills to pump water out of their flood-prone lowlands. The well-drained, sandy soil that resulted—along with the Dutch maritime climate—provided the perfect conditions for growing tulips, which arrived in Holland from Asia Minor in the late 1500s.

MARCH

S	M	T	W	T	F	S
	1	2	3	4	5	6
7	8	9	10	11	12	13
14	15	16	17	18	19	20
21	22	23	24	25	26	27
28	29	30	31			

APRIL

S	M	T	W	T	F	S
				1	2	3
4	5	6	7	8	9	10
11	12	13	14	15	16	17
18	19	20	21	22	23	24
25	26	27	28	29	30	

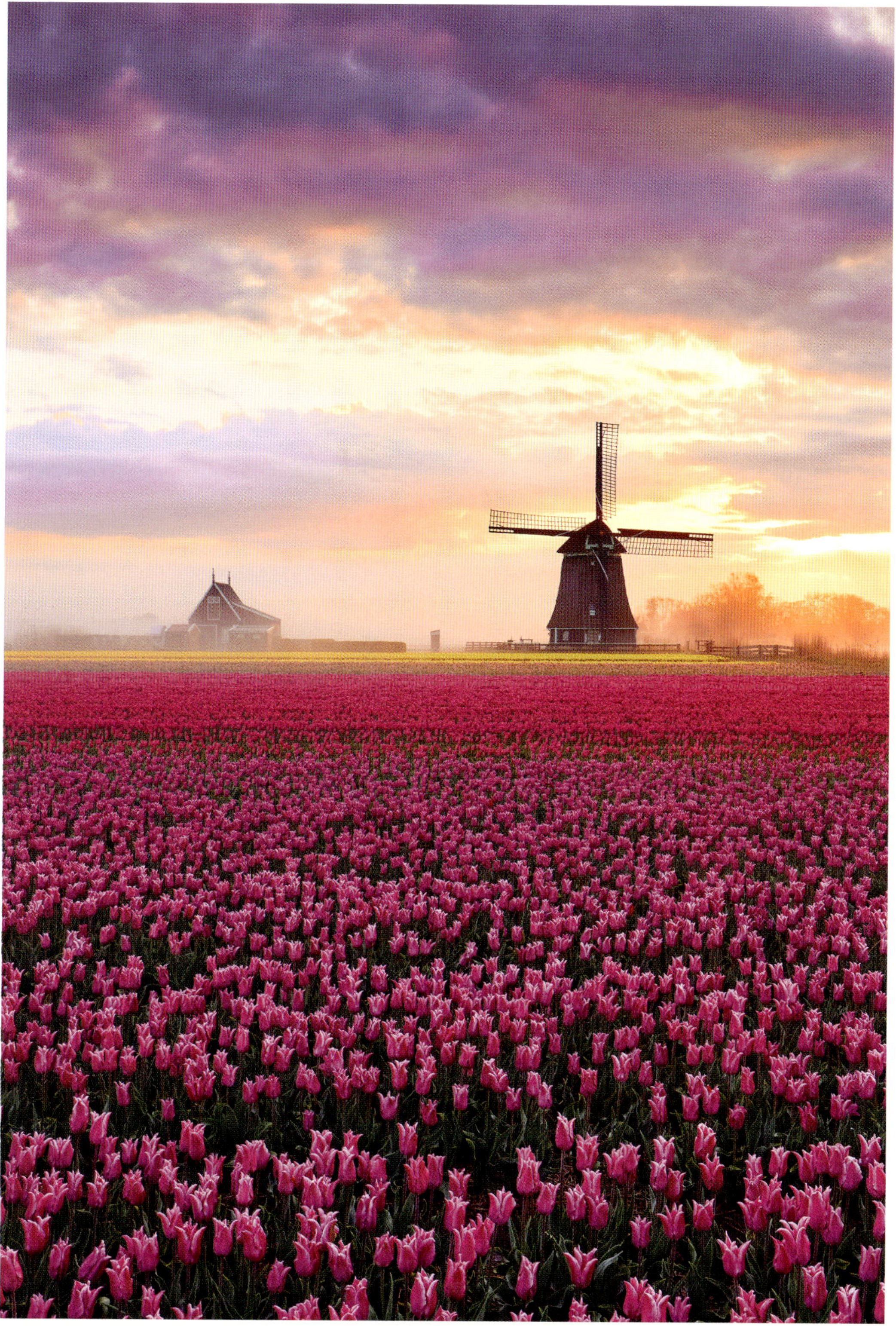

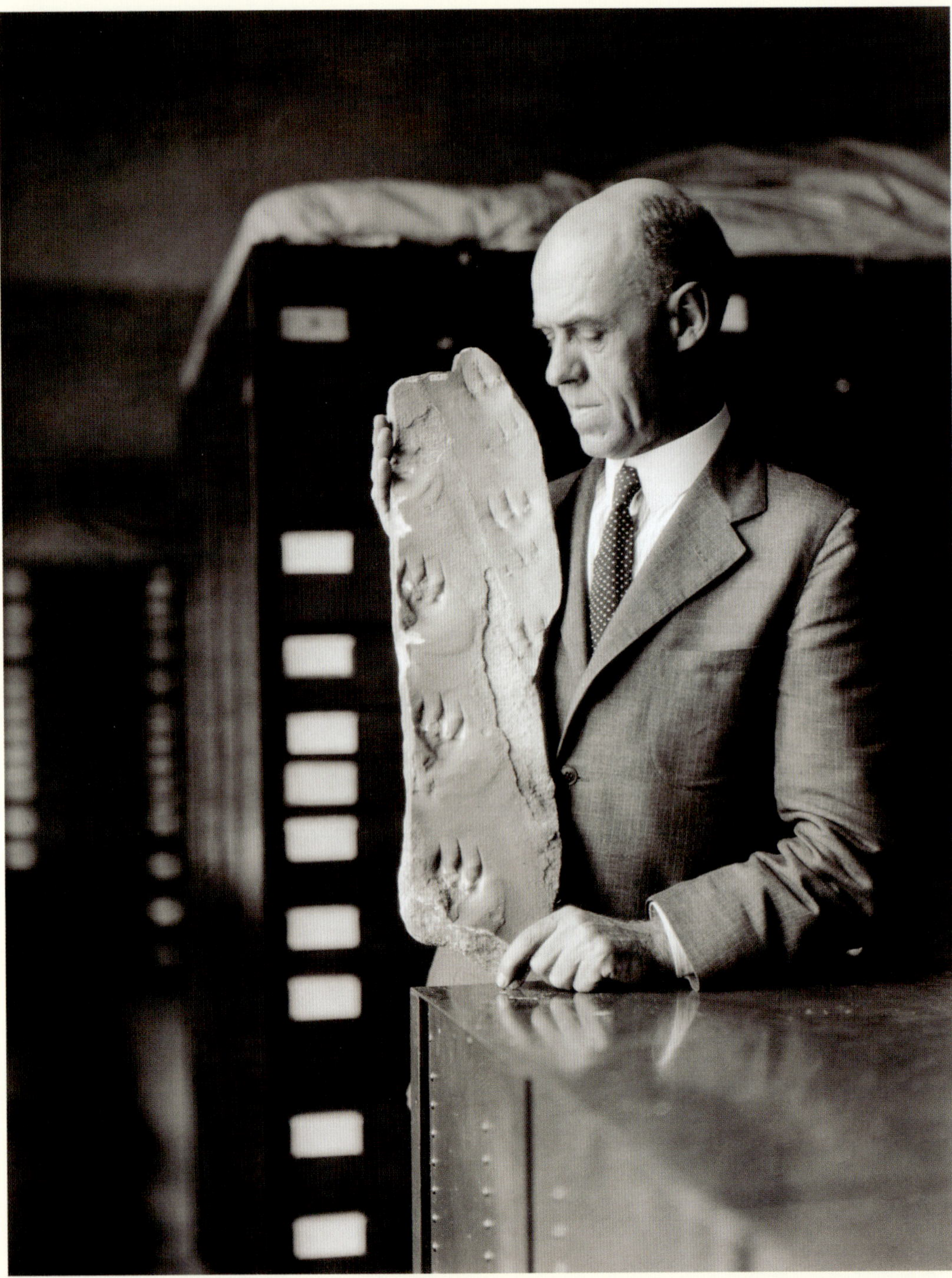

Charles Whitney Gilmore
with fossil, 1928
Gelatin silver print
Smithsonian Libraries
and Archives

Gilmore (1874–1945) was the curator of the division of vertebrate paleontology at the United States National Museum—now the National Museum of Natural History. He was a renowned paleontologist who published extensively and named many dinosaurs in North America. Here, Gilmore holds fossilized footprints of a prehistoric reptile.

APRIL

S	M	T	W	T	F	S
				1	2	3
4	5	6	7	8	9	10
11	12	13	14	15	.16	17
18	19	20	21	22	23	24
25	26	27	28	29	30	

MAY

S	M	T	W	T	F	S
						1
2	3	4	5	6	7	8
9	10	11	12	13	14	15
16	17	18	19	20	21	22
23	24	25	26	27	28	29
30	31					

APRIL

SUNDAY
4

MONDAY
5

● TUESDAY
6

WEDNESDAY
7

THURSDAY
8

FRIDAY
9

SATURDAY
10

APRIL

SUNDAY

11

MONDAY

12

TUESDAY ◐

13

WEDNESDAY

14

THURSDAY

15

FRIDAY

16

SATURDAY

17

Lemur leaf frog
(*Agalychnis lemur*)
Digital photograph by
Roshan Patel, August 2024
Washington, DC
Smithsonian's National
Zoo and Conservation
Biology Institute

Named for their large, striking eyes that recall the small primate of Madagascar, lemur leaf frogs have vertical pupils, enabling these nocturnal animals to see well in the dark. When the sun comes up, they tuck themselves onto the underside of leaves. Their dorsal coloring—a vibrant green—blends in perfectly, camouflaging them while they sleep.

APRIL

S	M	T	W	T	F	S
				1	2	3
4	5	6	7	8	9	10
11	12	13	14	15	16	17
18	19	20	21	22	23	24
25	26	27	28	29	30	

MAY

S	M	T	W	T	F	S
						1
2	3	4	5	6	7	8
9	10	11	12	13	14	15
16	17	18	19	20	21	22
23	24	25	26	27	28	29
30	31					

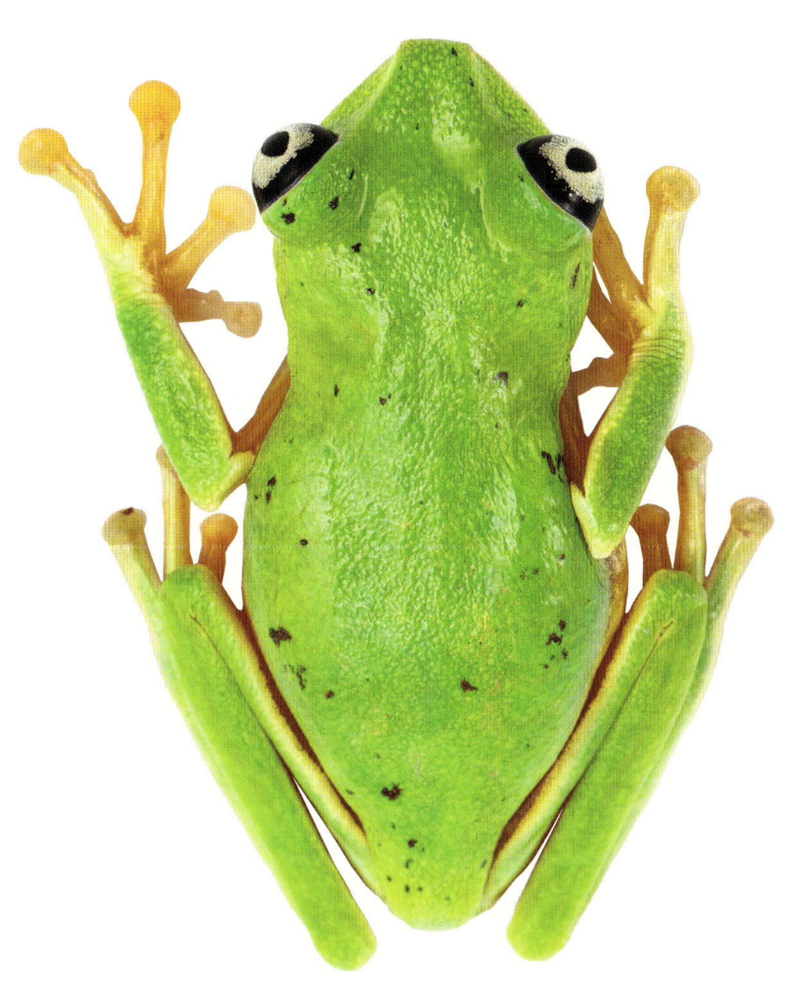

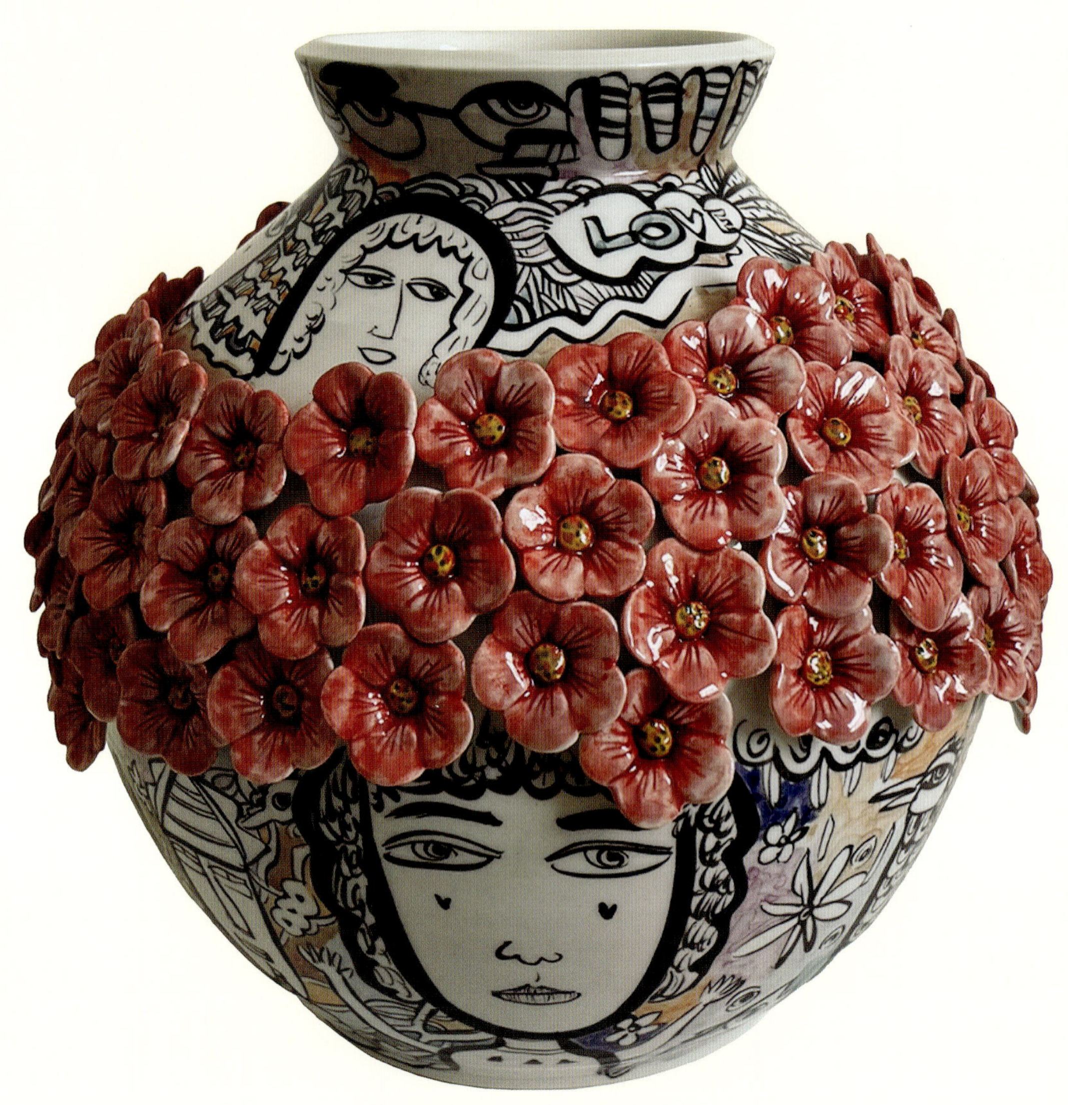

APRIL

Yeonsoo Kim
(b. South Korea, 1977)
Relationship Goal/
Flower Moon Jar, 2024
Porcelain, underglaze, glaze
11 × 12 in. (28 × 30.5 cm)
Smithsonian Craft Show

This piece by the New Hampshire–based Kim features a diverse array of likenesses and graffiti-like images that interact to suggest possible stories. The title nods to moon jars, an iconic type of traditional Korean ceramics.

SUNDAY

18

MONDAY

19

○

TUESDAY

20

PASSOVER BEGINS (SUNDOWN)

WEDNESDAY

21

EARTH DAY

THURSDAY

22

FRIDAY

23

SATURDAY

24

APRIL

S	M	T	W	T	F	S
				1	2	3
4	5	6	7	8	9	10
11	12	13	14	15	16	17
18	19	20	21	22	23	24
25	26	27	28	29	30	

MAY

S	M	T	W	T	F	S
						1
2	3	4	5	6	7	8
9	10	11	12	13	14	15
16	17	18	19	20	21	22
23	24	25	26	27	28	29
30	31					

APRIL · MAY

SUNDAY

25

MONDAY

26

TUESDAY

27

WEDNESDAY ◑

28

THURSDAY PASSOVER ENDS (SUNDOWN)

29

FRIDAY

30

SATURDAY

1

Apiculture trade card, late 19th century
Color lithograph on cardstock
5½ × 3⅜ in.
(14 cm × 8.6 cm)
Warshaw Collection of Business Americana
Archives Center, National Museum of American History

Illustrated trade cards—like this one marketing honey sold by Massachusetts merchant Charles Eldredge—were commonly used to advertise businesses and products in the late 1800s. The Warshaw Collection of Business Americana covers almost 500 topics from accounting to zoology and is the most used collection in the National Museum of American History's Archives Center.

APRIL

S	M	T	W	T	F	S
				1	2	3
4	5	6	7	8	9	10
11	12	13	14	15	16	17
18	19	20	21	22	23	24
25	26	27	28	29	30	

MAY

S	M	T	W	T	F	S
						1
2	3	4	5	6	7	8
9	10	11	12	13	14	15
16	17	18	19	20	21	22
23	24	25	26	27	28	29
30	31					

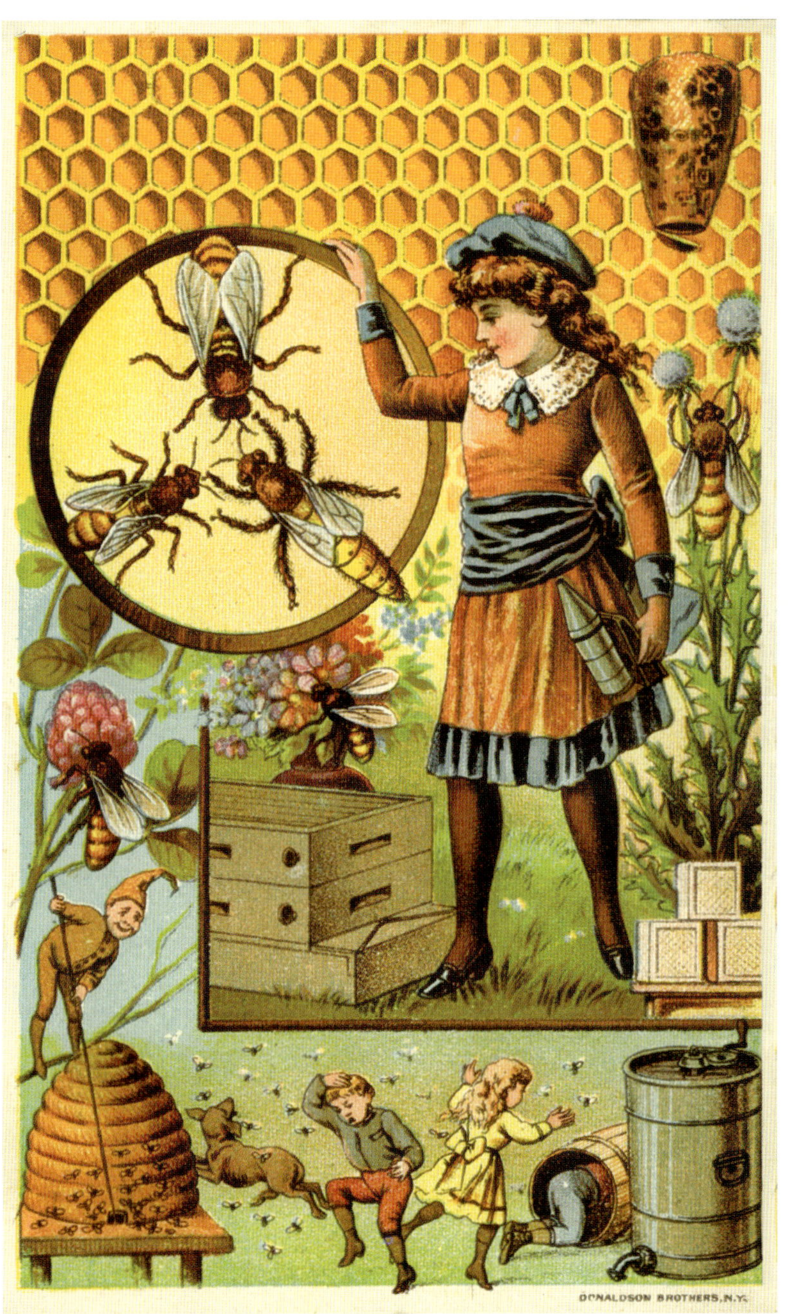
DONALDSON BROTHERS, N.Y.

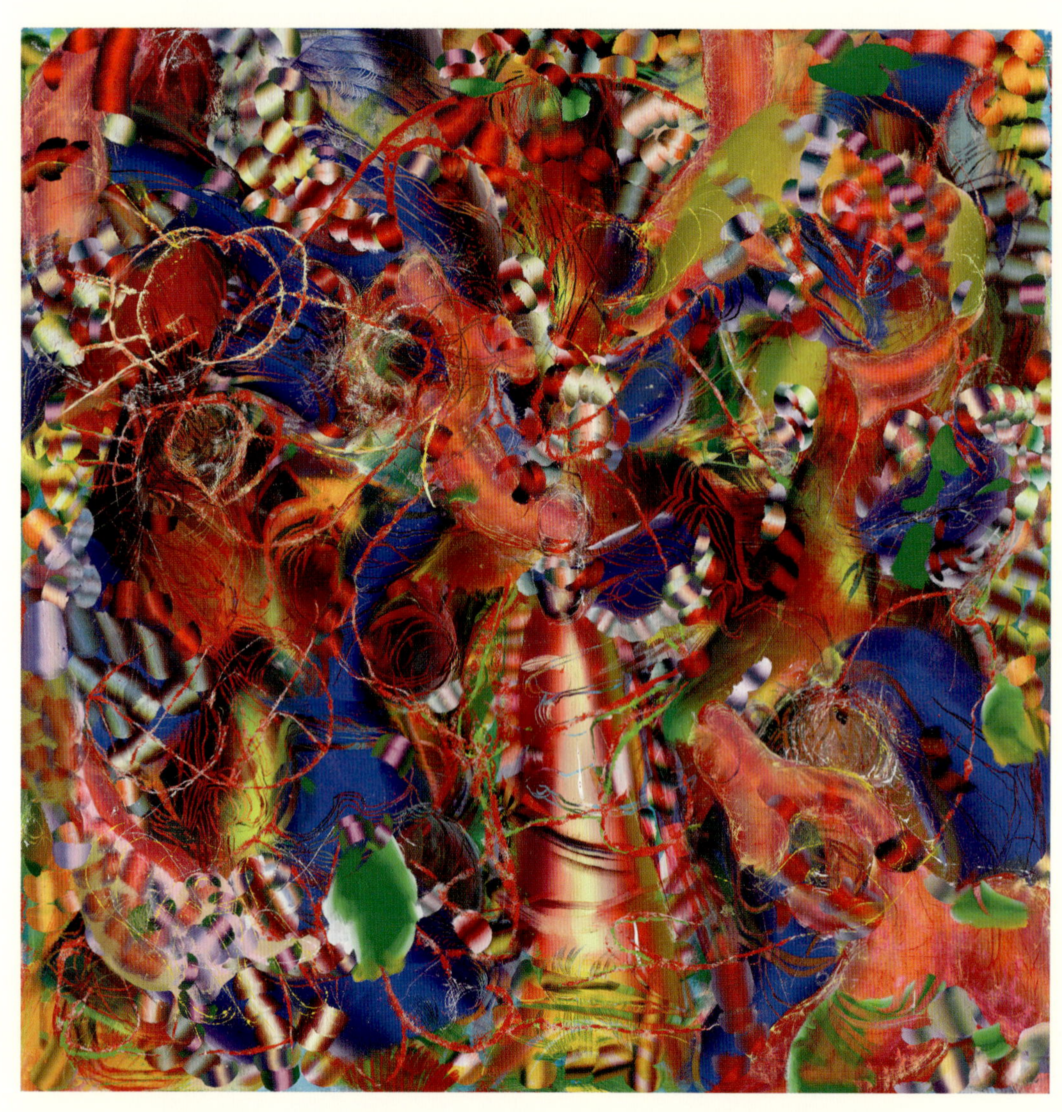

MAY

Lauren Quin (b. 1992)
Red Thread, 2022
Oil on canvas
72 × 72⅛ × 1⅜ in.
(182.9 × 183.2 × 3.5 cm)
Gift of Iris and Adam Singer
Hirshhorn Museum
and Sculpture Garden

Pulsing with vibrant color and sinuous shapes, Lauren Quin's densely layered paintings are inspired by the artist's experience of moving with a flashlight through pitch-black deep woods in Maine during an artist residency in 2017. In *Red Thread*, Quin's flash-light beam is depicted as a luminous tubular form (a motif borrowed from Cubist painter Fernand Léger) that slices through the center of the composition.

ORTHODOX EASTER

SUNDAY

2

MONDAY

3

TUESDAY

4

CINCO DE MAYO

WEDNESDAY

5

●

THURSDAY

6

FRIDAY

7

SATURDAY

8

MAY

S	M	T	W	T	F	S
						1
2	3	4	5	6	7	8
9	10	11	12	13	14	15
16	17	18	19	20	21	22
23	24	25	26	27	28	29
30	31					

JUNE

S	M	T	W	T	F	S
		1	2	3	4	5
6	7	8	9	10	11	12
13	14	15	16	17	18	19
20	21	22	23	24	25	26
27	28	29	30			

MAY

SUNDAY — MOTHER'S DAY

9

MONDAY

10

TUESDAY

11

WEDNESDAY

12

THURSDAY ◐

13

FRIDAY

14

SATURDAY

15

Purse, 1920s
Beadwork by Mary Elizabeth Jenkinson (n.d.)
Frame by Grace Hazen (1874–1940)
Glass-bead embroidery, silk velvet, engraved metal
15⅞ × 9½ × 1½ in.
(40.3 × 23.5 × 3.8 cm)
Gift of Gwendolyn Sauvage
Cooper Hewitt, Smithsonian Design Museum

The design of this bag was inspired by the textiles of the Byzantine empire and includes leaping gazelles and a tree with heart-shaped leaves and cascading blue flowers. The intricately beaded morning glory vine border was likely inspired by Jenkinson's own garden.

MAY

S	M	T	W	T	F	S
						1
2	3	4	5	6	7	8
9	10	11	12	13	14	15
16	17	18	19	20	21	22
23	24	25	26	27	28	29
30	31					

JUNE

S	M	T	W	T	F	S
		1	2	3	4	5
6	7	8	9	10	11	12
13	14	15	16	17	18	19
20	21	22	23	24	25	26
27	28	29	30			

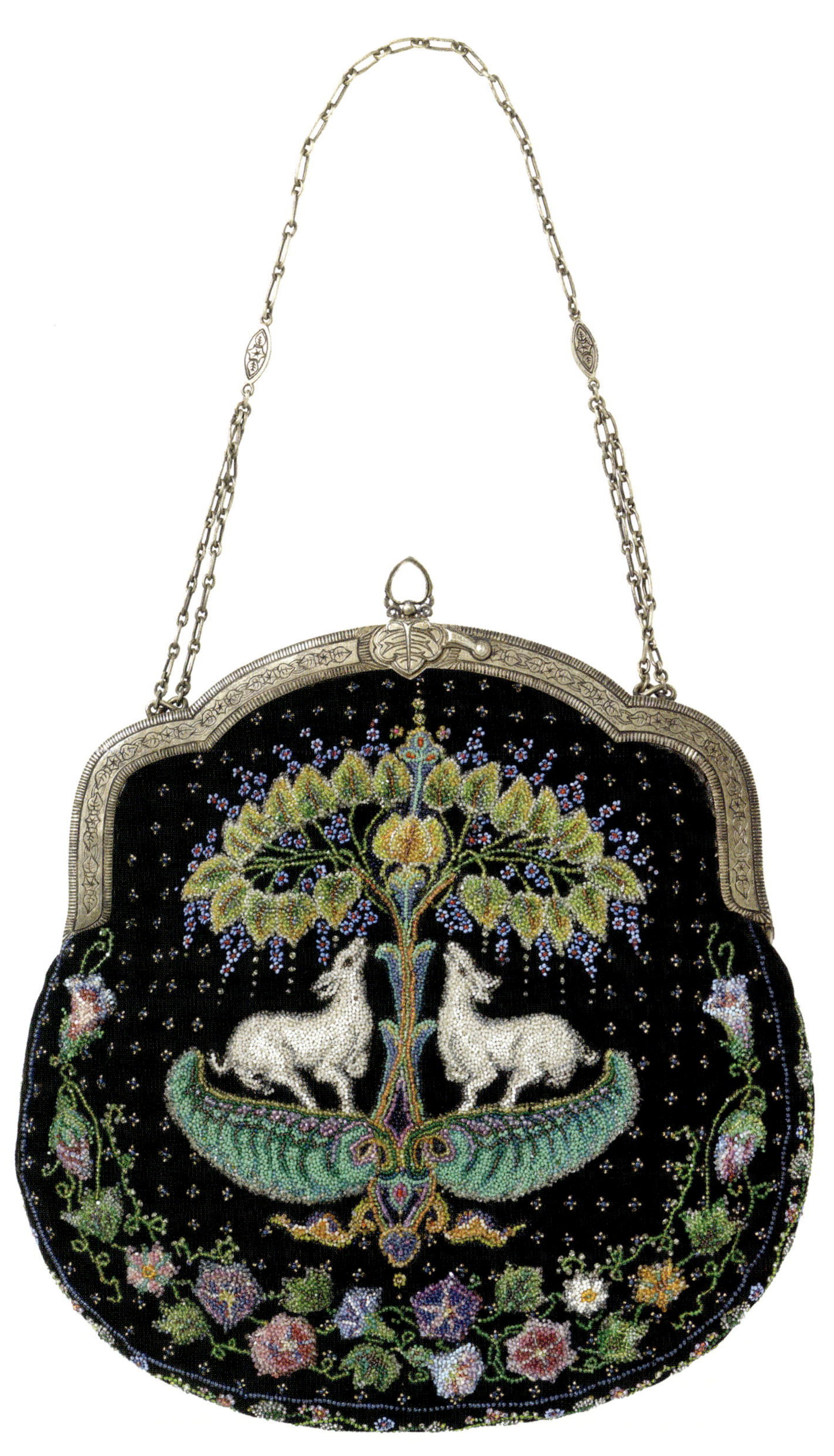

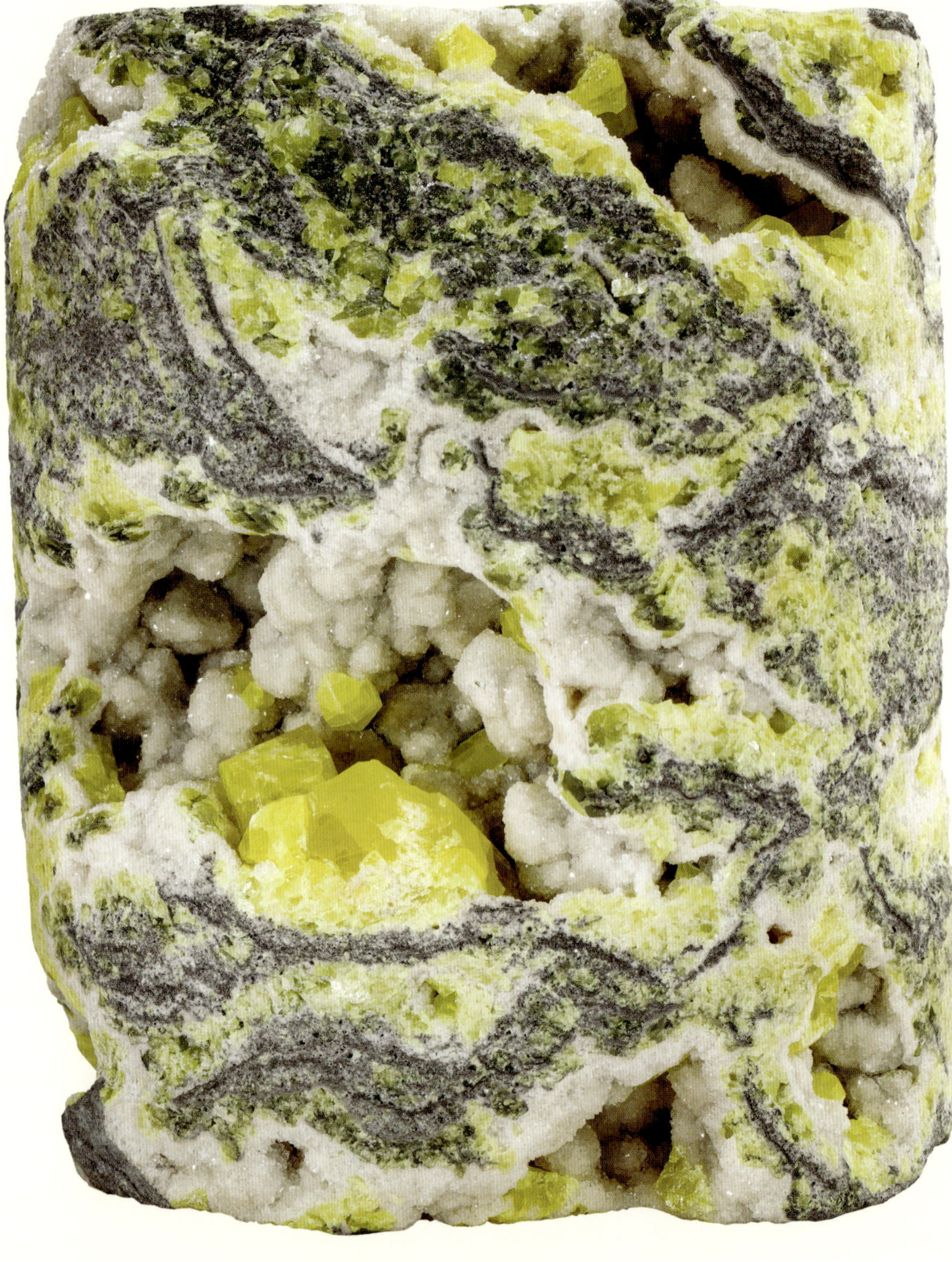

MAY

Sulfur with Celestine
Texas
6¼ × 5 in. (15.8 × 12.6 cm)
National Museum
of Natural History

This core sample features bright yellow sulfur crystals together with white celestine. The fifth most abundant element on the planet, sulfur is essential to support all life and is critical in volcanic and deep-Earth processes. It has also been called "brimstone" due to its flammability and is often associated with the odor of rotten eggs.

SUNDAY
16
EID AL-ADHA BEGINS (SUNDOWN)

MONDAY
17
EID AL-ADHA ENDS (SUNDOWN)

TUESDAY
18

WEDNESDAY
19

THURSDAY
20
○

FRIDAY
21

SATURDAY
22

MAY

S	M	T	W	T	F	S
						1
2	3	4	5	6	7	8
9	10	11	12	13	14	15
16	17	18	19	20	21	22
23	24	25	26	27	28	29
30	31					

JUNE

S	M	T	W	T	F	S
		1	2	3	4	5
6	7	8	9	10	11	12
13	14	15	16	17	18	19
20	21	22	23	24	25	26
27	28	29	30			

MAY

SUNDAY

23

MONDAY

VICTORIA DAY (CAN.)

24

TUESDAY

25

WEDNESDAY

26

THURSDAY

27

FRIDAY

◑

28

SATURDAY

29

Can of Seacrest brand oysters, 1935–50
H. B. Kennerly & Son Inc., Nanticoke, MD
Ink on paper, metal
7⅜ × 6⅝ × 6⅝ in.
(18.7 × 16.8 × 16.8 cm)
National Museum of African American History and Culture

From the 1870s to the 1970s African American men earned a living on the Chesapeake Bay fishing and gathering oysters. They would sell their harvests to seafood processing plants, where (primarily) African American women shucked and canned the oysters for sale in other markets.

MAY

S	M	T	W	T	F	S
						1
2	3	4	5	6	7	8
9	10	11	12	13	14	15
16	17	18	19	20	21	22
23	24	25	26	27	28	29
30	31					

JUNE

S	M	T	W	T	F	S
		1	2	3	4	5
6	7	8	9	10	11	12
13	14	15	16	17	18	19
20	21	22	23	24	25	26
27	28	29	30			

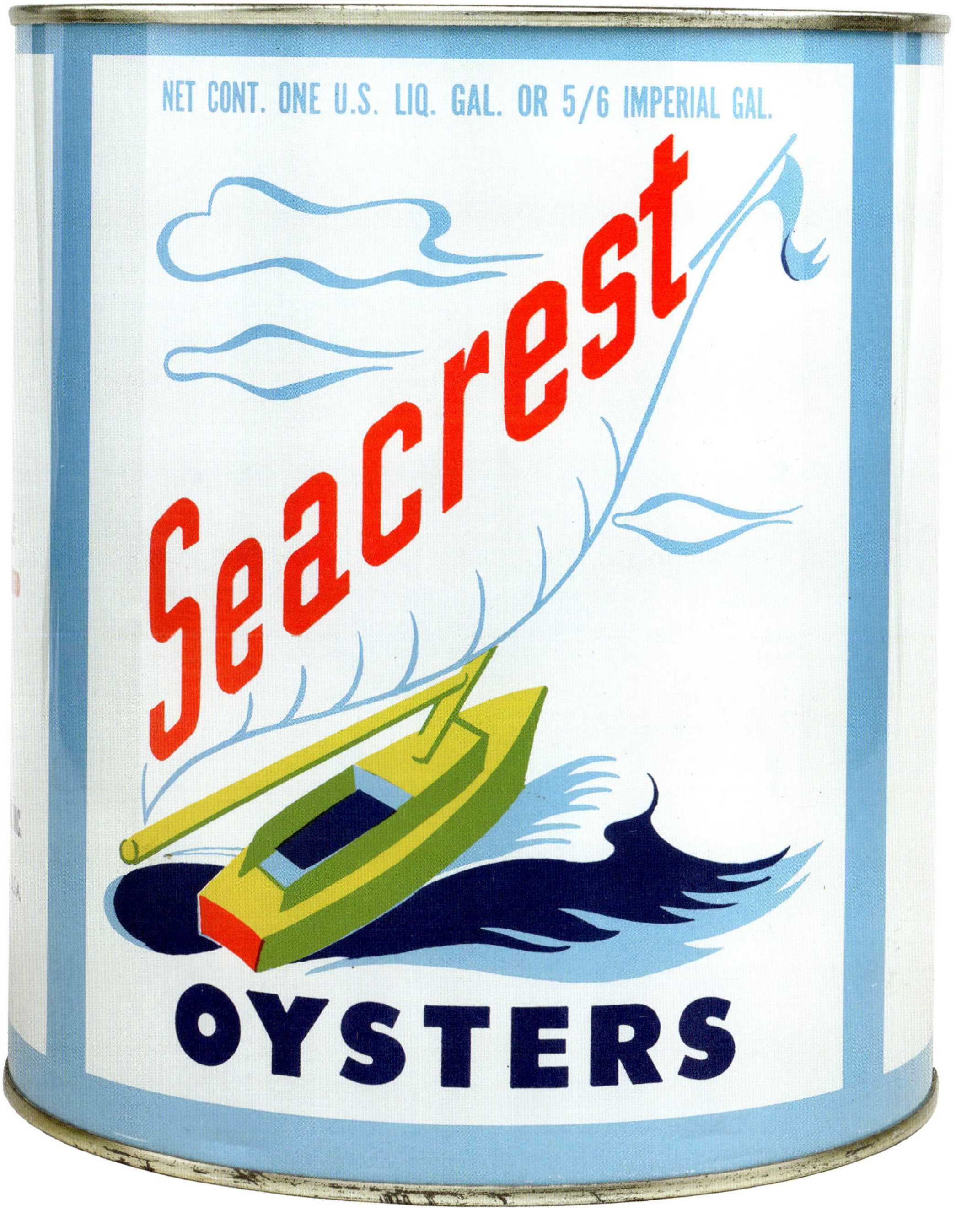

NET CONT. ONE U.S. LIQ. GAL. OR 5/6 IMPERIAL GAL.

Seacrest

OYSTERS

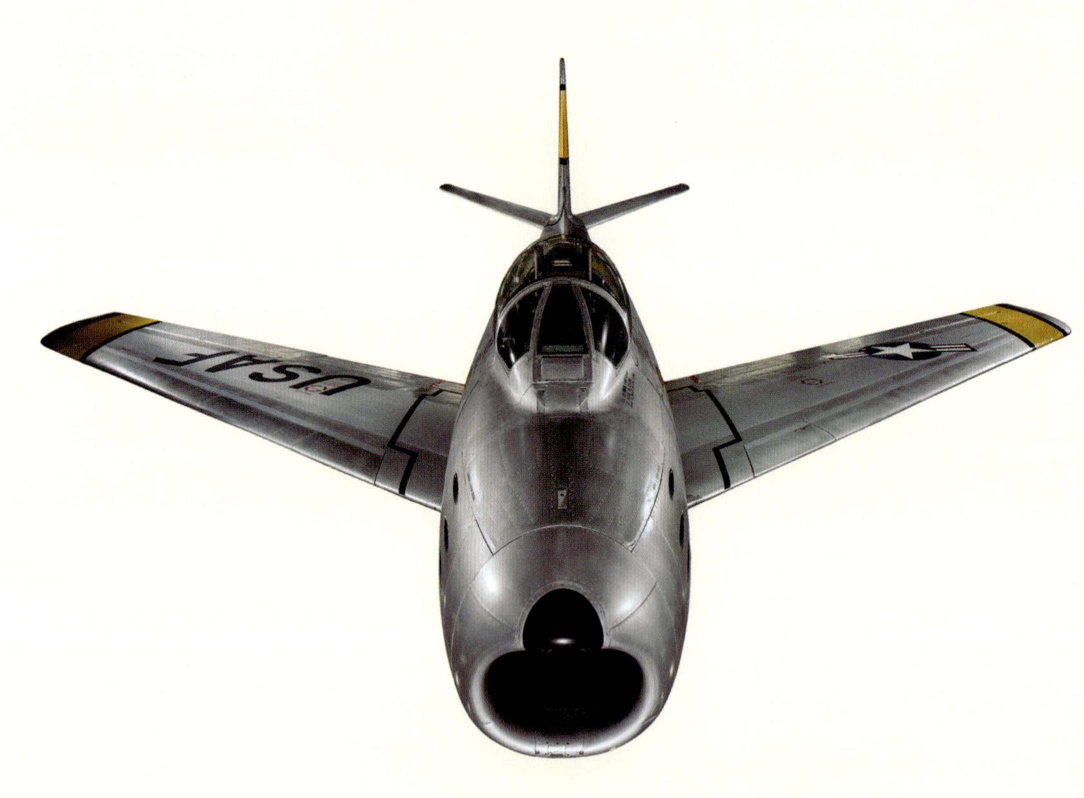
USAF

MAY • JUNE

F-86 Sabre, 1947
North American Aviation, Los Angeles
14 ft. 9 in. × 37 ft. 6 in. (450 × 1,143 cm)
National Air and Space Museum

The F-86 Sabre was the first American swept-wing fighter. With wings that were angled back from the fuselage rather than perpendicular to it, the F-86 Sabre could be controlled at much higher speeds than its straight-wing counterparts. Sabres played an important role in the Korean War, flying missions to shoot down enemy MiG-15 fighters.

SUNDAY
30

MEMORIAL DAY

MONDAY
31

TUESDAY
1

WEDNESDAY
2

THURSDAY
3

●

FRIDAY
4

MUHARRAM BEGINS (SUNDOWN)

SATURDAY
5

MAY

S	M	T	W	T	F	S
						1
2	3	4	5	6	7	8
9	10	11	12	13	14	15
16	17	18	19	20	21	22
23	24	25	26	27	28	29
30	31					

JUNE

S	M	T	W	T	F	S
		1	2	3	4	5
6	7	8	9	10	11	12
13	14	15	16	17	18	19
20	21	22	23	24	25	26
27	28	29	30			

JUNE

SUNDAY

6

MONDAY

7

TUESDAY

8

WEDNESDAY

9

THURSDAY

10

FRIDAY

◐

11

SATURDAY

12

Los Angeles Angels baseball jersey worn by Shohei Ohtani, 2023
Nike Inc., Beaverton, OR
Polyester, ink
35 × 38 in. (89 × 96.5 cm)
National Museum of American History

On July 27, 2023, Shohei Ohtani of the Los Angeles Angels wore this jersey in a double-header against the Detroit Tigers. In the first contest, the groundbreaking athlete from Japan threw a complete-game, one-hit shutout; in the second, he moved to the outfield and hit two home runs. In 2024 the multitime All-Star joined the Los Angeles Dodgers, and in 2025 he won his fourth Most Valuable Player award.

JUNE

S	M	T	W	T	F	S
		1	2	3	4	5
6	7	8	9	10	11	12
13	14	15	16	17	18	19
20	21	22	23	24	25	26
27	28	29	30			

JULY

S	M	T	W	T	F	S
				1	2	3
4	5	6	7	8	9	10
11	12	13	14	15	16	17
18	19	20	21	22	23	24
25	26	27	28	29	30	31

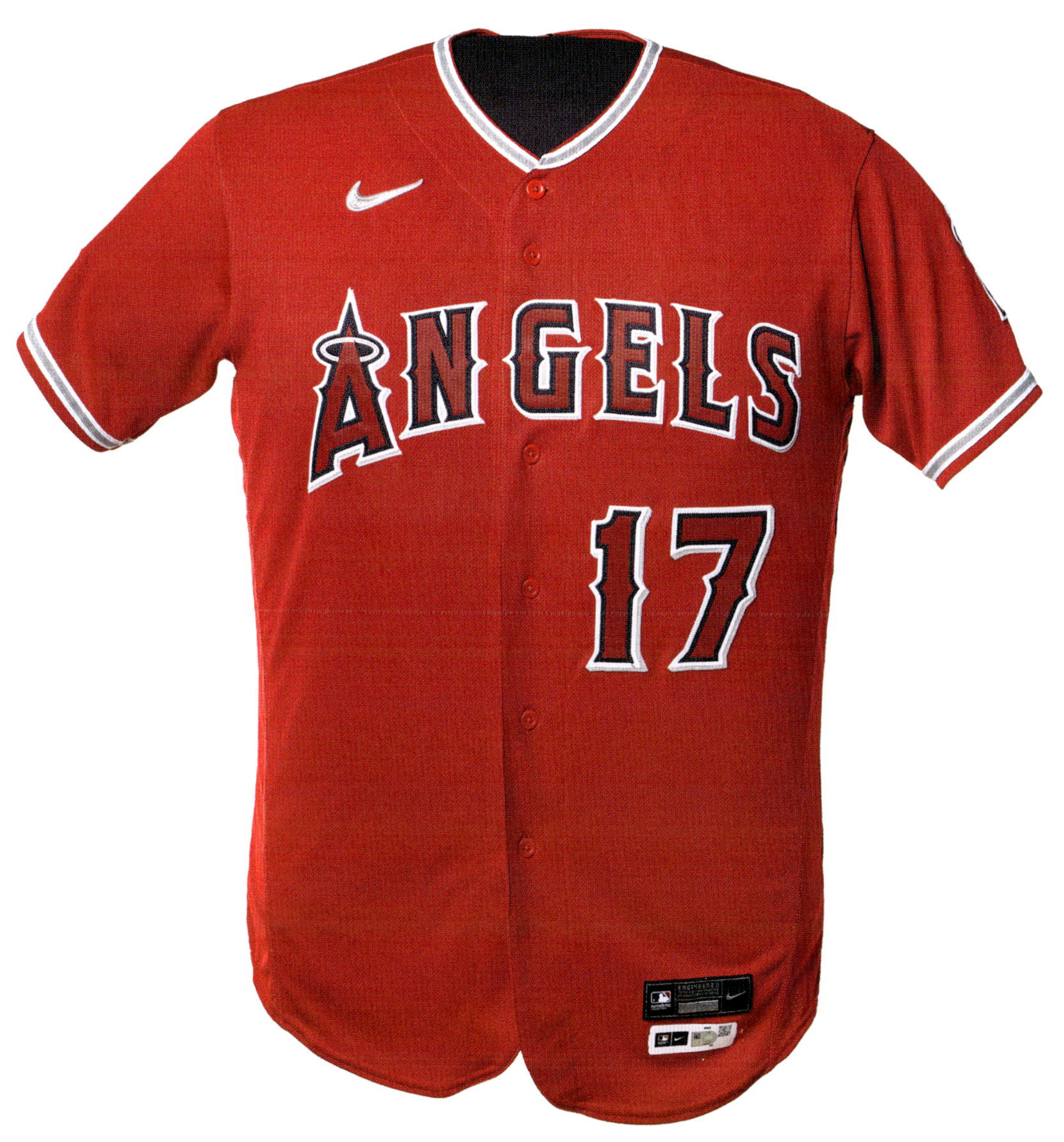
ANGELS
17

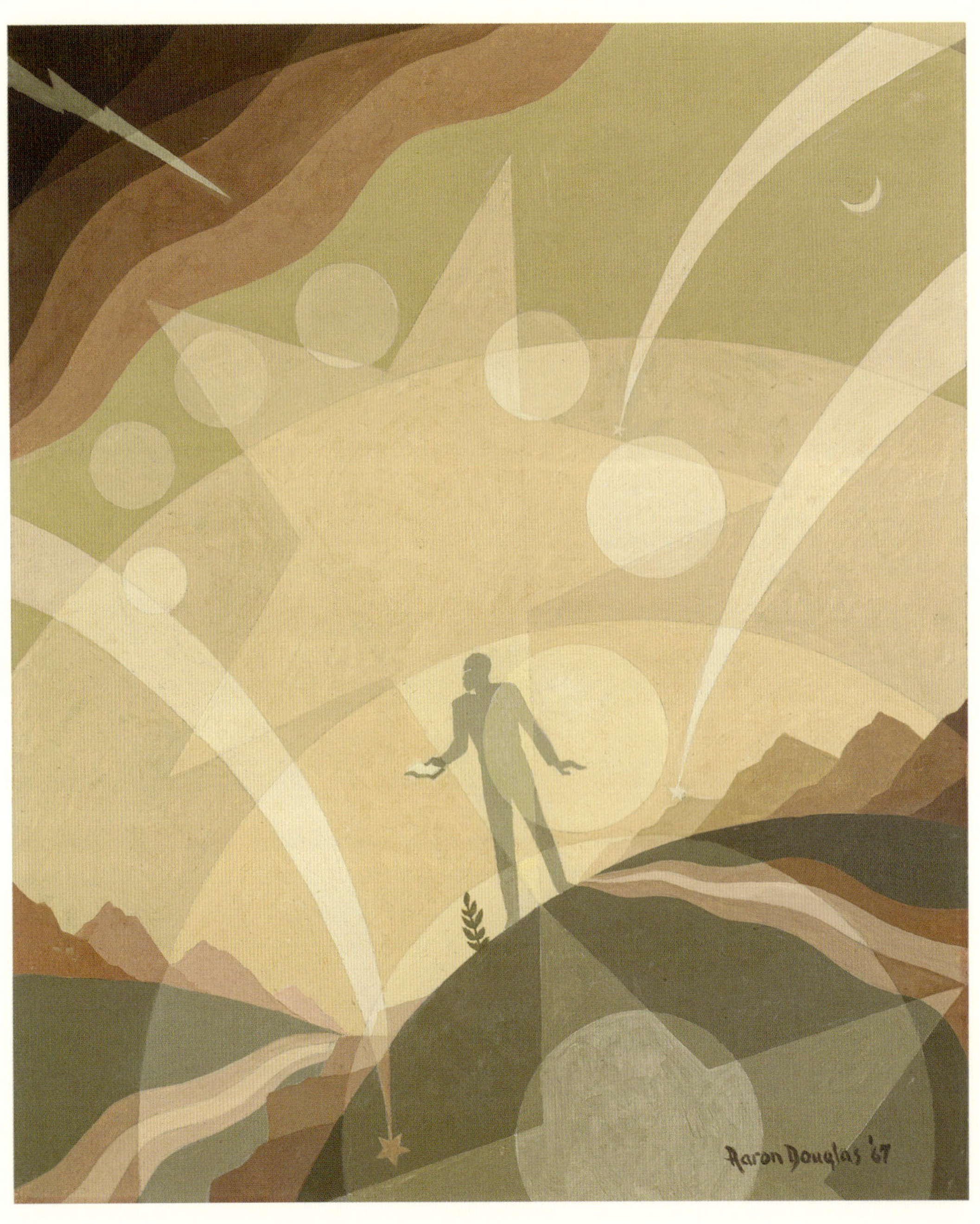
Aaron Douglas '67

Aaron Douglas (1899–1979)
Inspiration, 1967
Oil on canvas panel
30 × 25 in. (76 × 63.5 cm)
Gift of Steven L. Jones
in memory of his father
Dr. William M. Jones Sr.,
Chicago educator and
a storyteller for the soul
Smithsonian American
Art Museum

Douglas's style fused European modernism and African imagery and motifs. The artist studied with the German émigré Winold Reiss, who encouraged him to explore his African roots in his art. *Inspiration* depicts a silhouetted figure holding a book, gazing toward the sky, and appearing to absorb creative energy from the cubist-inspired background.

JUNE

SUNDAY
13

FLAG DAY

MONDAY
14

TUESDAY
15

WEDNESDAY
16

THURSDAY
17

○

FRIDAY
18

JUNETEENTH

SATURDAY
19

JUNE

S	M	T	W	T	F	S
		1	2	3	4	5
6	7	8	9	10	11	12
13	14	15	16	17	18	19
20	21	22	23	24	25	26
27	28	29	30			

JULY

S	M	T	W	T	F	S
				1	2	3
4	5	6	7	8	9	10
11	12	13	14	15	16	17
18	19	20	21	22	23	24
25	26	27	28	29	30	31

JUNE

SUNDAY — FATHER'S DAY

20

MONDAY — FIRST DAY OF SUMMER

21

TUESDAY

22

WEDNESDAY

23

THURSDAY

24

FRIDAY

25

SATURDAY

26

Pippa Garner (1942–2024)
Thinkman cabinet, 1984
Polyurethane finish on plywood and white wood filler, hardwood legs, cabinet hardware, electrical wiring and hardware, galvanized sheet metal
59 × 23½ × 9½ in.
(150 × 59 × 24 cm)
Cooper Hewitt, Smithsonian Design Museum

Thinkman parodies consumer culture and American masculinity with a flashing, peek-a-boo gesture that transforms a suit-jacket silhouette into a satirical cabinet. The work is a rare example of Garner's early explorations in fashion, design, and performance and was constructed from parts of an earlier work, *Permafashion Sports Jacket*.

JUNE

S	M	T	W	T	F	S
		1	2	3	4	5
6	7	8	9	10	11	12
13	14	15	16	17	18	19
20	21	22	23	24	25	26
27	28	29	30			

JULY

S	M	T	W	T	F	S
				1	2	3
4	5	6	7	8	9	10
11	12	13	14	15	16	17
18	19	20	21	22	23	24
25	26	27	28	29	30	31

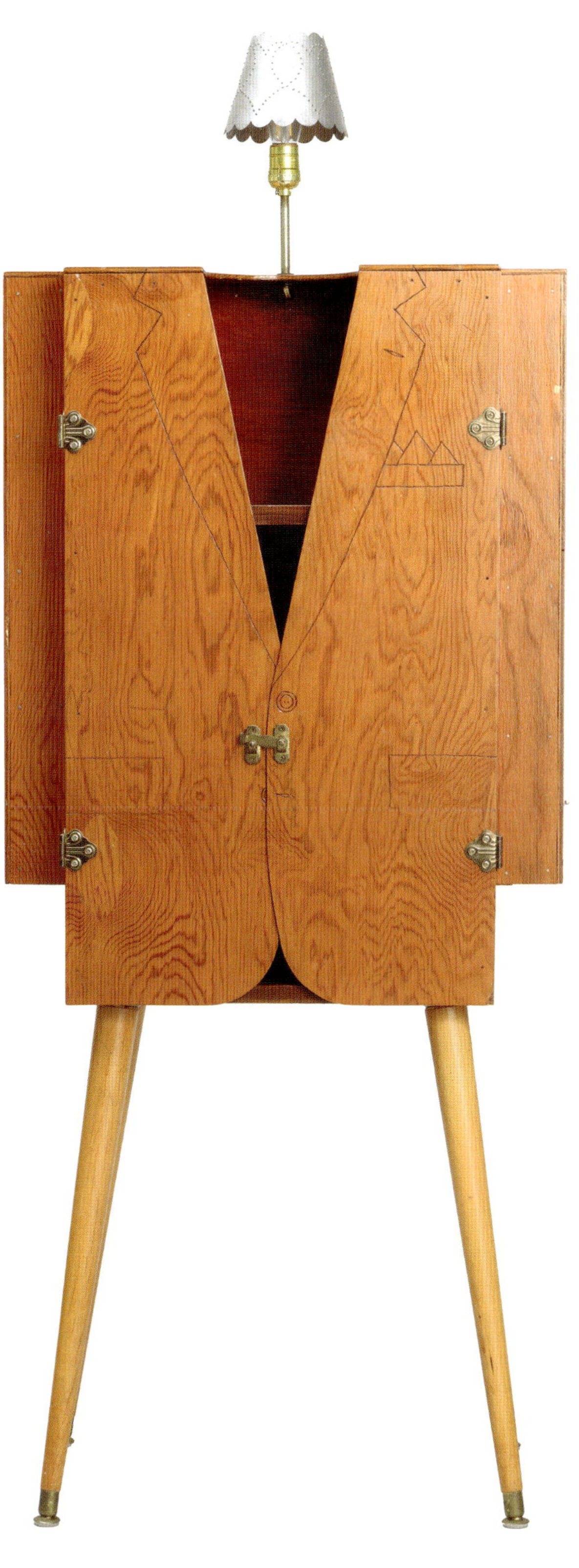

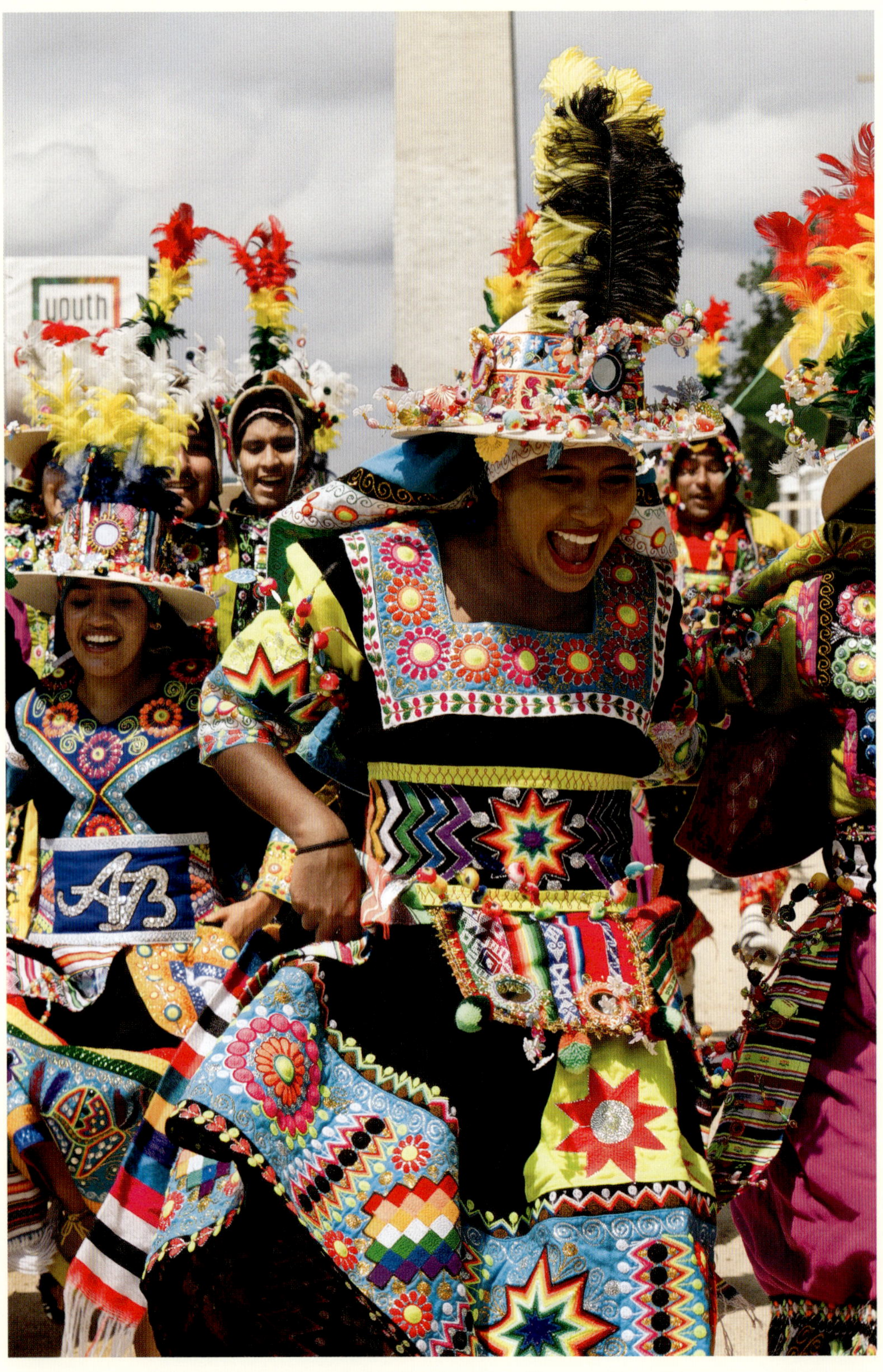
youth
AB

JUNE • JULY

Bolivian Americans from the Washington, DC, region perform at the 2025 Smithsonian Folklife Festival
Digital photograph by Sonya Pencheva, July 6, 2025
National Mall, Washington, DC
Smithsonian Center for Folklife and Cultural Heritage

In the Quechua language, *tinkuy* means "to come together." At the 2025 Smithsonian Folklife Festival, young Bolivian Americans came together on the National Mall to perform *el baile del tinku*, a folk dance honoring Pachamama, Mother Earth in Indigenous Andean cosmology.

◑ SUNDAY 27

MONDAY 28

TUESDAY 29

WEDNESDAY 30

CANADA DAY

THURSDAY 1

FRIDAY 2

● SATURDAY 3

JUNE

S	M	T	W	T	F	S
		1	2	3	4	5
6	7	8	9	10	11	12
13	14	15	16	17	18	19
20	21	22	23	24	25	26
27	28	29	30			

JULY

S	M	T	W	T	F	S
				1	2	3
4	5	6	7	8	9	10
11	12	13	14	15	16	17
18	19	20	21	22	23	24
25	26	27	28	29	30	31

JULY

SUNDAY

4

INDEPENDENCE DAY

MUHARRAM ENDS (SUNDOWN)

MONDAY

5

TUESDAY

6

WEDNESDAY

7

THURSDAY

8

FRIDAY

9

SATURDAY ◐

10

20¢ USA and Jet airmail stamp
1968
Paper, ink, adhesive
1 × 1⁹⁄₁₆ in. (2.5 × 4 cm)
National Postal Museum

Debuting in 1918, US airmail service expedited mail delivery and required higher postage than standard surface mail. This 1968 airmail stamp cost 20¢ compared to a 6¢ regular stamp at the time. As mail was increasingly transported via airplane, the higher domestic airmail rate was largely discontinued in 1975.

JULY

S	M	T	W	T	F	S
				1	2	3
4	5	6	7	8	9	10
11	12	13	14	15	16	17
18	19	20	21	22	23	24
25	26	27	28	29	30	31

AUGUST

S	M	T	W	T	F	S
1	2	3	4	5	6	7
8	9	10	11	12	13	14
15	16	17	18	19	20	21
22	23	24	25	26	27	28
29	30	31				

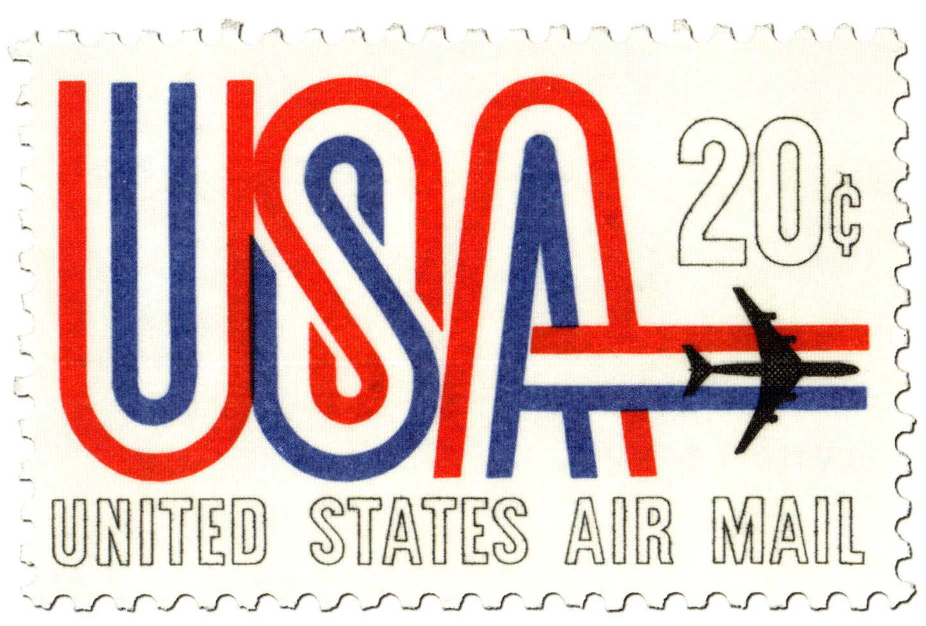
USA
20¢
UNITED STATES AIR MAIL

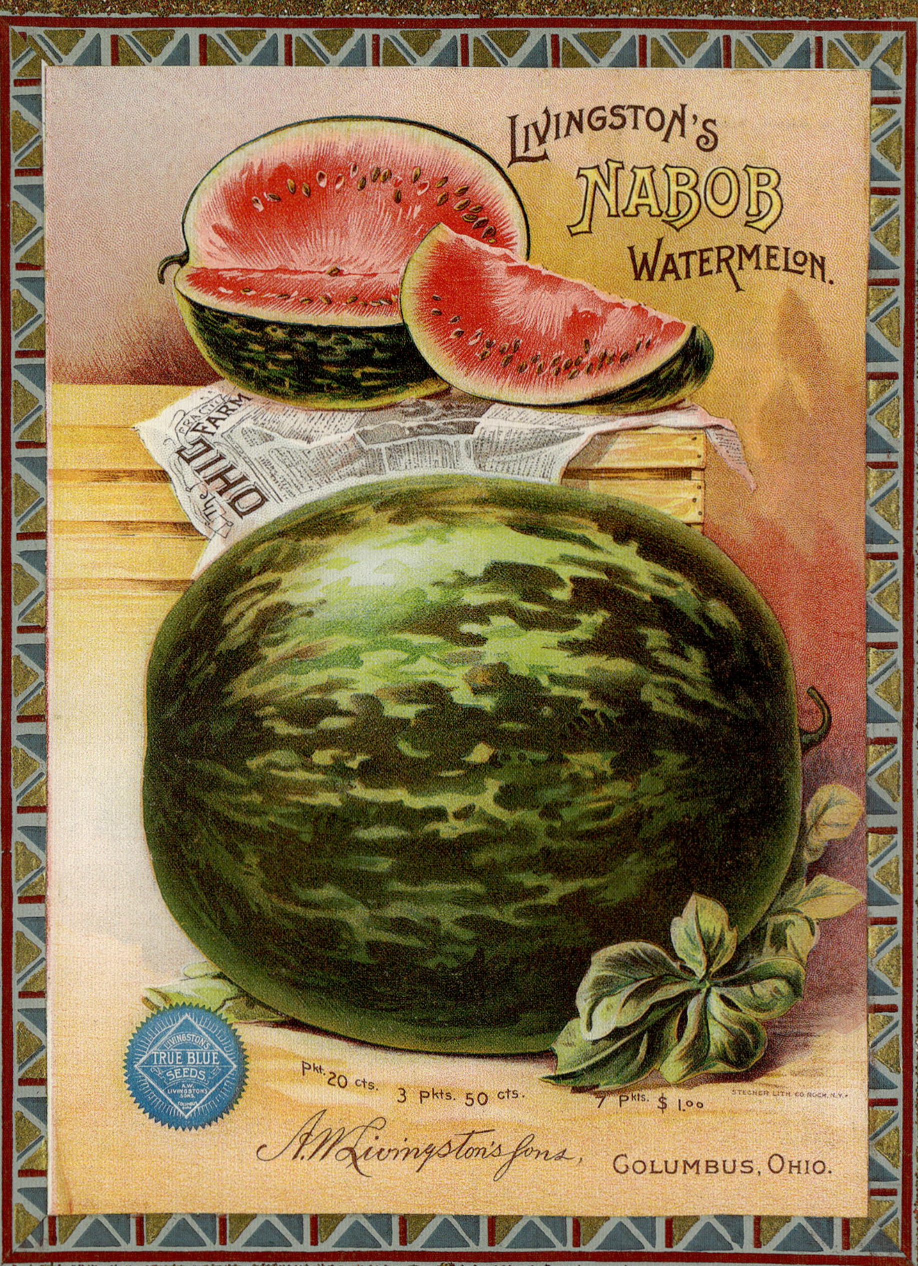

LIVINGSTON'S
NABOB
WATERMELON.
OHIO FARM
LIVINGSTON'S
TRUE BLUE
SEEDS.
A.W.
LIVINGSTON'S
SONS.
Pkt. 20 cts. 3 Pkts. 50 cts. 7 Pkts. $ 1.00
STECHER LITH. CO. ROCH. N.Y.
A. W. Livingston's Sons, COLUMBUS, OHIO.

Front cover of Livingston's True Blue Seeds catalog, c. 1891–1904
A. W. Livingston's Sons, Columbus, OH
Ink, paper mounted on cardboard
11¾ × 8¹¹⁄₁₆ in. (29.8 × 22.1 cm)
Horticultural Artifacts Collection
Smithsonian Gardens

This bright and bold seed catalog cover showcases the marketing of heirloom varieties—in this case, Livingston's Nabob Watermelon. A glimpse into America's horticultural past, it reflects the artistry and innovation of seed companies. These catalogs were more than sales tools; they were cultural artifacts that captured America's agricultural spirit.

JULY

S	M	T	W	T	F	S
				1	2	3
4	5	6	7	8	9	10
11	12	13	14	15	16	17
18	19	20	21	22	23	24
25	26	27	28	29	30	31

AUGUST

S	M	T	W	T	F	S
1	2	3	4	5	6	7
8	9	10	11	12	13	14
15	16	17	18	19	20	21
22	23	24	25	26	27	28
29	30	31				

JULY

SUNDAY

11

MONDAY

12

TUESDAY

13

WEDNESDAY

14

THURSDAY

15

FRIDAY

16

SATURDAY

17

JULY

SUNDAY

18

MONDAY

19

TUESDAY

20

WEDNESDAY

21

THURSDAY

22

FRIDAY

23

SATURDAY

24

Simon George Mpata
(Tanzanian, 1942–1984)
Untitled, 1971–73
Enamel paint on fiberboard
24¼ × 24¼ in.
(61.6 × 61.6 cm)
Gift of Ambassador and
Mrs. W. Beverly Carter Jr.
National Museum
of African Art

Mpata's painting style is often called Tinga Tinga, a reference to his half-brother Edward Tingatinga, who organized self-taught artists in Dar es Salaam, Tanzania. Distinguished by bright colors, the paintings by this group primarily focus on animals arrayed in curvilinear decorative patterns—as in this fisherman scene set on Africa's east coast.

JULY

S	M	T	W	T	F	S
				1	2	3
4	5	6	7	8	9	10
11	12	13	14	15	16	17
18	19	20	21	22	23	24
25	26	27	28	29	30	31

AUGUST

S	M	T	W	T	F	S
1	2	3	4	5	6	7
8	9	10	11	12	13	14
15	16	17	18	19	20	21
22	23	24	25	26	27	28
29	30	31				

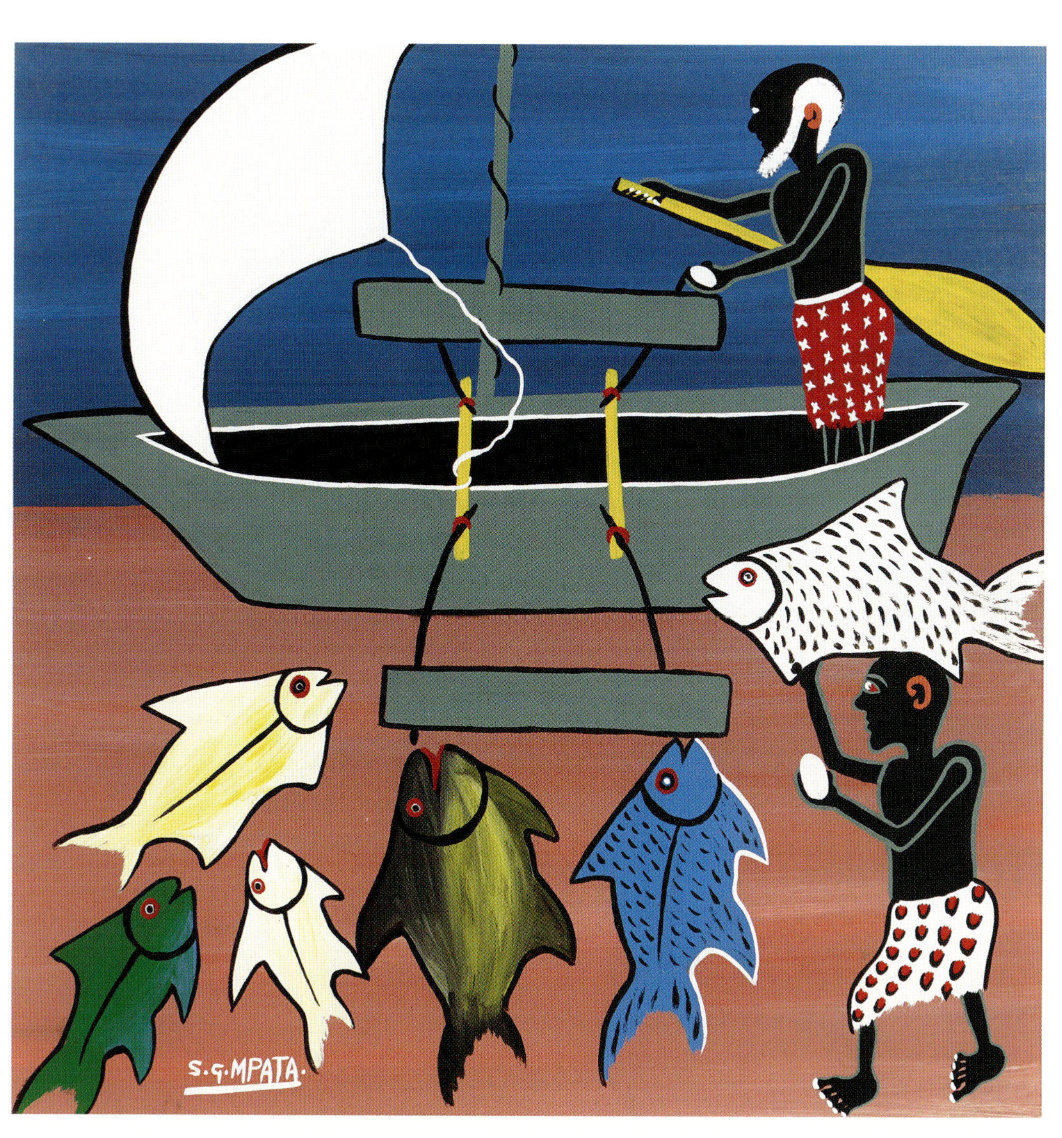
S.G.MPATA.

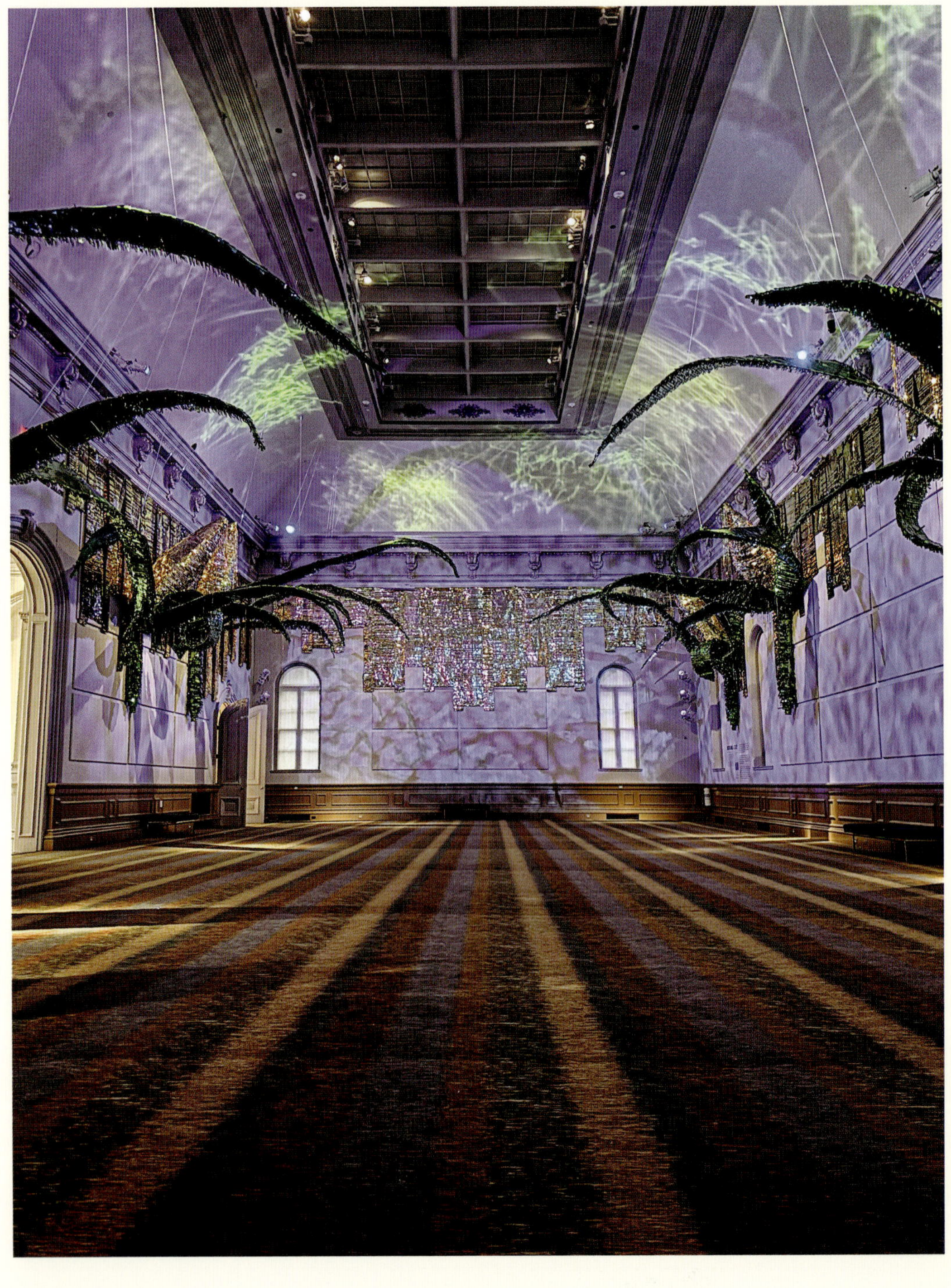

JULY

Justin Favela (b. 1986)
Capilla de Maíz
(Maize Chapel), 2025
Mixed media
Dimensions variable
Smithsonian American
Art Museum

Favela's mixed-media practice incorporates traditional Mexican and Latin American craft—specifically the papier-maché sculptures called *cartonería*—into large-scale sculptures and installations. *Capilla de Maíz (Maize Chapel)* honors the profound cultural significance of corn, or maize, which sustained Indigenous peoples and later European settlers in the Americas.

SUNDAY
25

◑

MONDAY
26

TUESDAY
27

WEDNESDAY
28

THURSDAY
29

FRIDAY
30

SATURDAY
31

JULY

S	M	T	W	T	F	S
				1	2	3
4	5	6	7	8	9	10
11	12	13	14	15	16	17
18	19	20	21	22	23	24
25	26	27	28	29	30	31

AUGUST

S	M	T	W	T	F	S
1	2	3	4	5	6	7
8	9	10	11	12	13	14
15	16	17	18	19	20	21
22	23	24	25	26	27	28
29	30	31				

AUGUST

SUNDAY

1

MONDAY

2

TUESDAY

3

WEDNESDAY

4

THURSDAY

5

FRIDAY

6

SATURDAY

7

Hi Yu Apples crate label, 1940s
Northern Fruit Co. Inc., Wenatchee, WA
Paper, ink
8¾ × 10½ in.
(22.2 × 26.7 cm)
Smithsonian Institution Traveling Exhibition Service

Before they were replaced by cardboard boxes in the 1960s, wooden crates bearing colorful labels were used to ship fruit and vegetables. Hi Yu—meaning "abundance" in the language of the Chinook people of the Pacific Northwest—was the name of a brand of apples shipped from Wenatchee, Washington. The traveling Museum on Main Street exhibition *Americans* explores how intertwined Native Americans are in the identity of the United States.

AUGUST

S	M	T	W	T	F	S
1	2	3	4	5	6	7
8	9	10	11	12	13	14
15	16	17	18	19	20	21
22	23	24	25	26	27	28
29	30	31				

SEPTEMBER

S	M	T	W	T	F	S
			1	2	3	4
5	6	7	8	9	10	11
12	13	14	15	16	17	18
19	20	21	22	23	24	25
26	27	28	29	30		

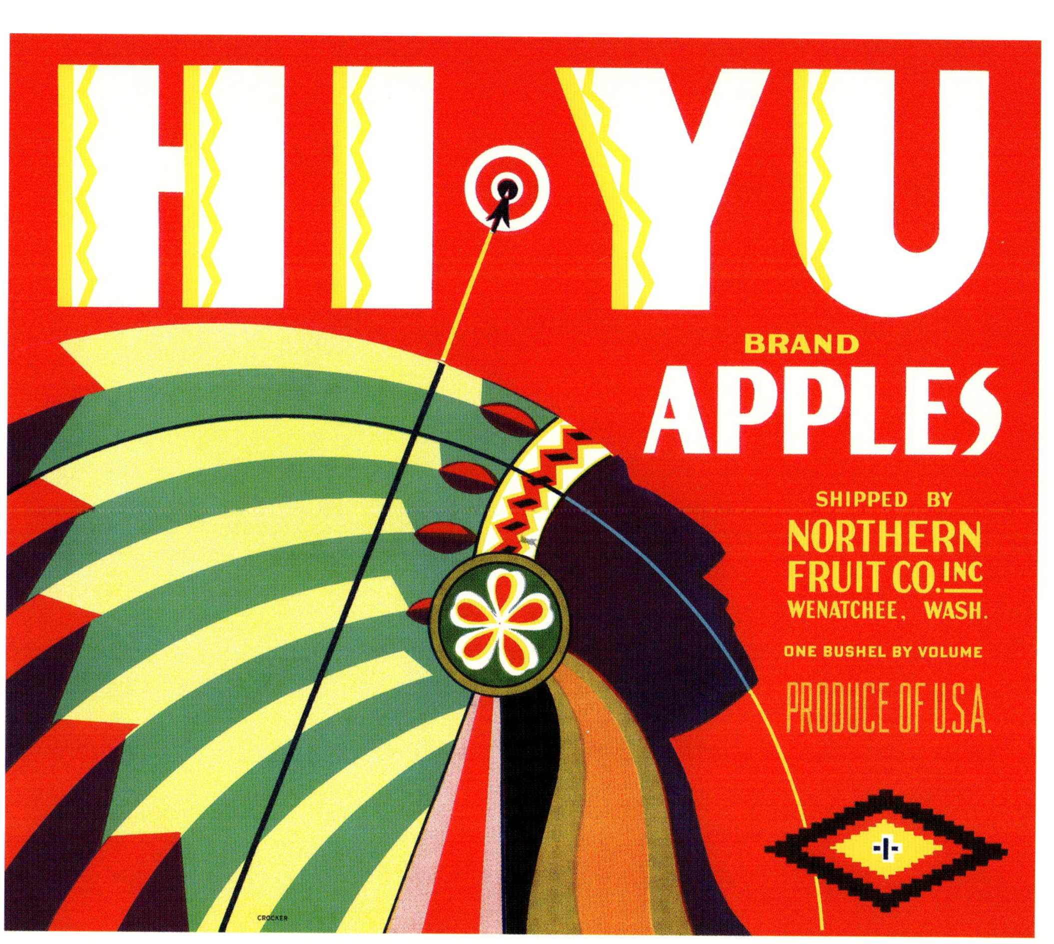
HI-YU
BRAND
APPLES
SHIPPED BY
NORTHERN
FRUIT CO. INC
WENATCHEE, WASH.
ONE BUSHEL BY VOLUME
PRODUCE OF U.S.A.

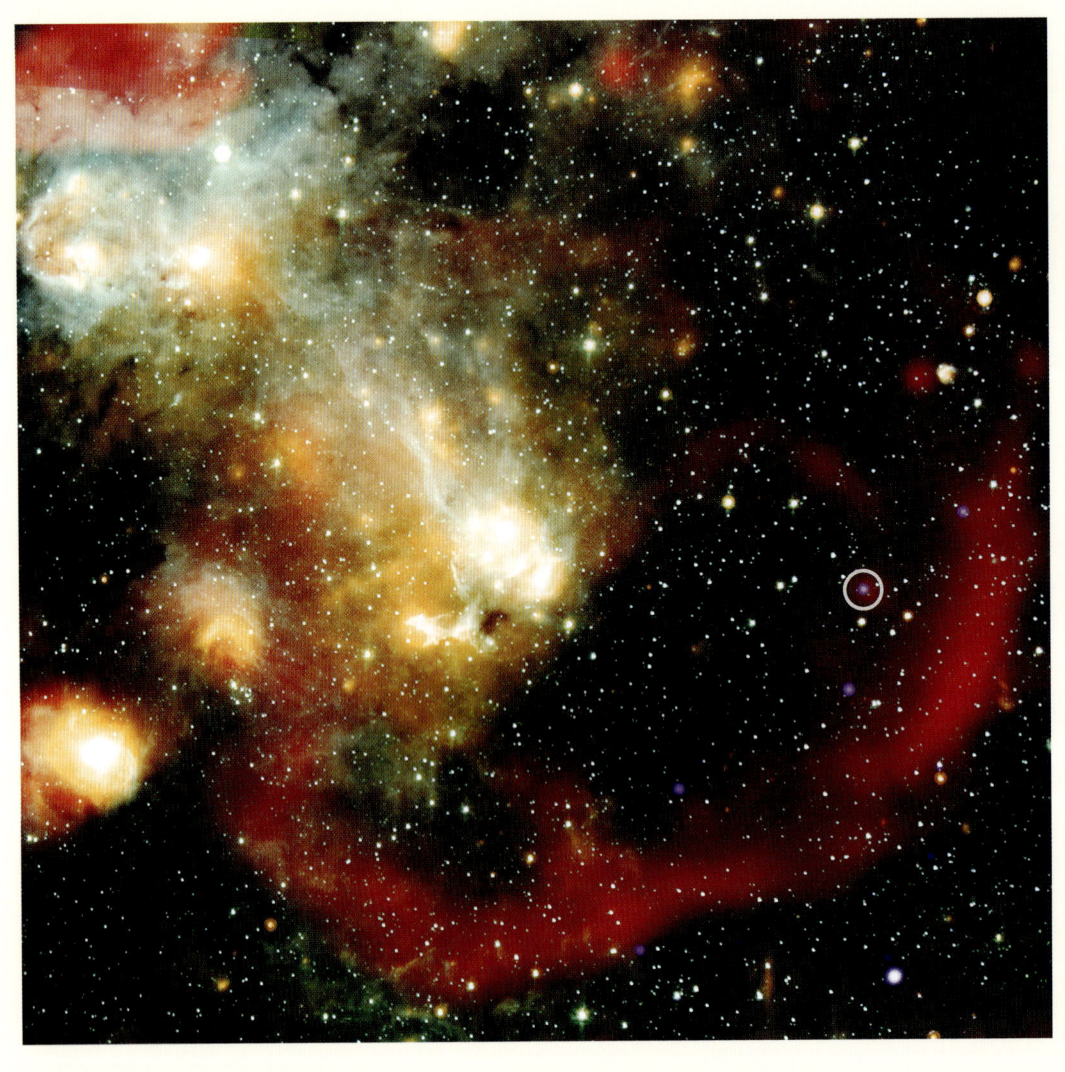

AUGUST

Wide-field image of ASKAP J1832 (circled) in X-ray, radio, and infrared light
Digital photograph made from X-rays detected by NASA's Chandra X-ray Observatory, infrared light detected by the Spitzer Space Telescope, and radio light detected by LOFAR, May 28, 2025
Chandra X-ray Observatory/Spitzer Space Telescope/LOFAR
Smithsonian Astrophysical Observatory

Scientists using the Chandra X-ray Observatory and other telescopes discovered a star behaving like no other seen before. The intensity of X-rays and radio waves from ASKAP J1832–0911 cycles every 44 minutes. This image of ASKAP and the surrounding area shows X-rays from the Chandra X-ray Observatory (blue), infrared data from the Spitzer Space Telescope (teal and orange), and radio light from LOFAR, or the Low-Frequency Array (red).

AUGUST

S	M	T	W	T	F	S
1	2	3	4	5	6	7
8	9	10	11	12	13	14
15	16	17	18	19	20	21
22	23	24	25	26	27	28
29	30	31				

SEPTEMBER

S	M	T	W	T	F	S
			1	2	3	4
5	6	7	8	9	10	11
12	13	14	15	16	17	18
19	20	21	22	23	24	25
26	27	28	29	30		

SUNDAY

8

◐

MONDAY

9

TUESDAY

10

WEDNESDAY

11

THURSDAY

12

FRIDAY

13

SATURDAY

14

AUGUST

SUNDAY

15

MONDAY

16

TUESDAY

17

WEDNESDAY

18

THURSDAY

19

FRIDAY

20

SATURDAY

21

Dorr Bothwell (1902–2000)
Sketchbook, c. 1975
Brush pen on paper
10⅝ × 8⅝ in. (27 × 22 cm)
Dorr Bothwell papers, 1900–2006
Archives of American Art

Bothwell was a California-born artist, designer, and educator who was a stalwart of the West Coast art scene. After building her chops with New Deal arts programs, she traveled the world with her sketchbook as a diary. This drawing comes from around 1975 as she toured the islands of the Pacific.

AUGUST

S	M	T	W	T	F	S
1	2	3	4	5	6	7
8	9	10	11	12	13	14
15	16	17	18	19	20	21
22	23	24	25	26	27	28
29	30	31				

SEPTEMBER

S	M	T	W	T	F	S
			1	2	3	4
5	6	7	8	9	10	11
12	13	14	15	16	17	18
19	20	21	22	23	24	25
26	27	28	29	30		

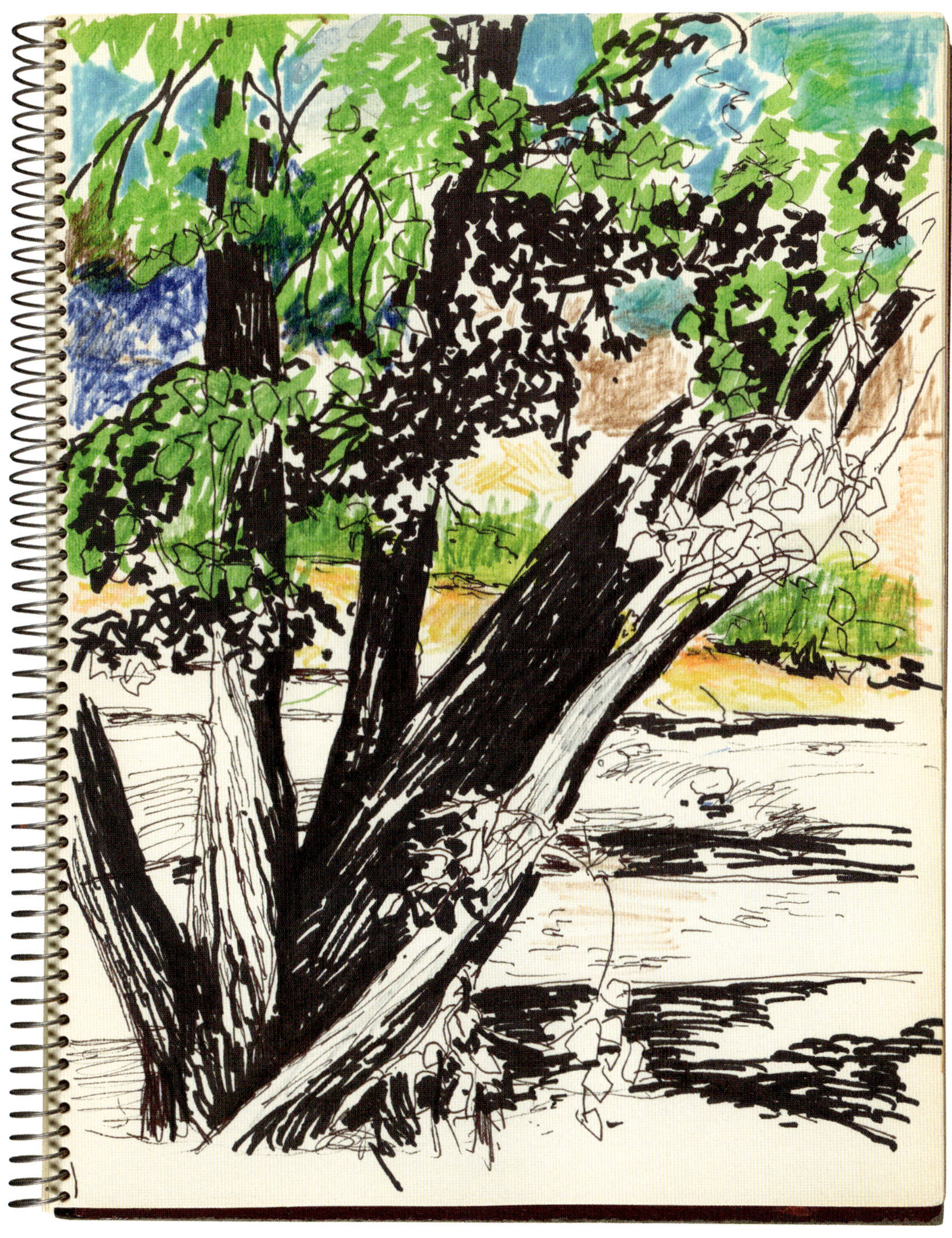

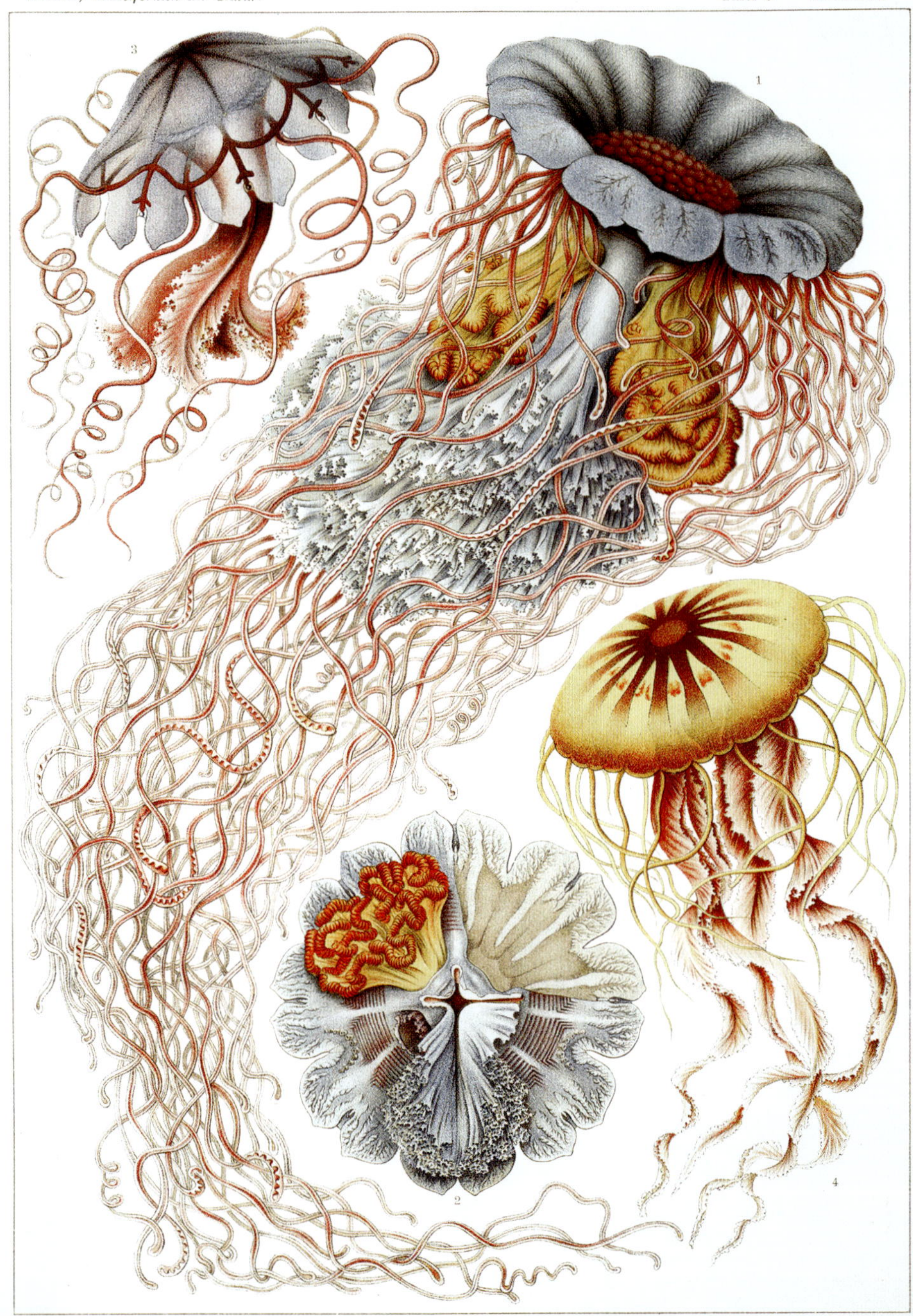

Discomedusae. — Scheibenquallen.

AUGUST

Ernst Haeckel
(German, 1834–1919)
Discomedusae from
Kunstformen der Natur, 1899
Ink on paper
14 × 10½ in.
(35.6 × 26.7 cm)
Smithsonian Libraries
and Archives

Authored by the German zoologist Ernst Haeckel, *Kunstformen der Natur* (*Art Forms in Nature*) was influential across numerous areas of study in the twentieth century, from the sciences to the arts. This plate from the book shows Discomedusae, a subclass of jellyfish.

SUNDAY
22

MONDAY
23

◑
TUESDAY
24

WEDNESDAY
25

THURSDAY
26

FRIDAY
27

SATURDAY
28

AUGUST

S	M	T	W	T	F	S
1	2	3	4	5	6	7
8	9	10	11	12	13	14
15	16	17	18	19	20	21
22	23	24	25	26	27	28
29	30	31				

SEPTEMBER

S	M	T	W	T	F	S
			1	2	3	4
5	6	7	8	9	10	11
12	13	14	15	16	17	18
19	20	21	22	23	24	25
26	27	28	29	30		

AUGUST · SEPTEMBER

SUNDAY

29

MONDAY

30

TUESDAY

31

WEDNESDAY

1

THURSDAY

2

FRIDAY

3

SATURDAY

4

Estevan Oriol (b. 1966)
Chill 57 Scrapin', 1990s, printed 2022
Inkjet print
16 × 20 in. (40.6 × 50.8 cm)
Museum purchase through the Smithsonian Latino Initiatives Pool, administered by the National Museum of the American Latino
National Museum of American History

A lowrider is customized with hydraulics to raise and lower the car and to make it appear to dance or hop—and express the personality of its owner. This 1957 Chevrolet Bel Air is lowered in the back and has a titanium plate that makes sparks when it scrapes the road as it cruises the boulevard.

AUGUST

S	M	T	W	T	F	S
1	2	3	4	5	6	7
8	9	10	11	12	13	14
15	16	17	18	19	20	21
22	23	24	25	26	27	28
29	30	31				

SEPTEMBER

S	M	T	W	T	F	S
			1	2	3	4
5	6	7	8	9	10	11
12	13	14	15	16	17	18
19	20	21	22	23	24	25
26	27	28	29	30		

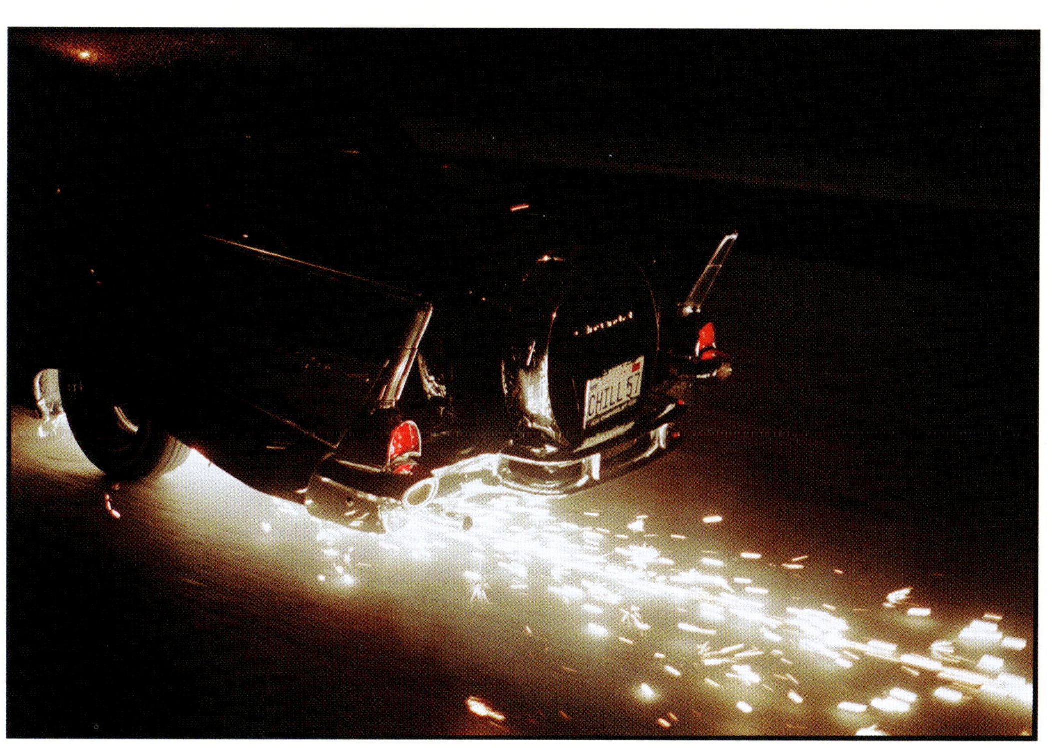
CHILL 57

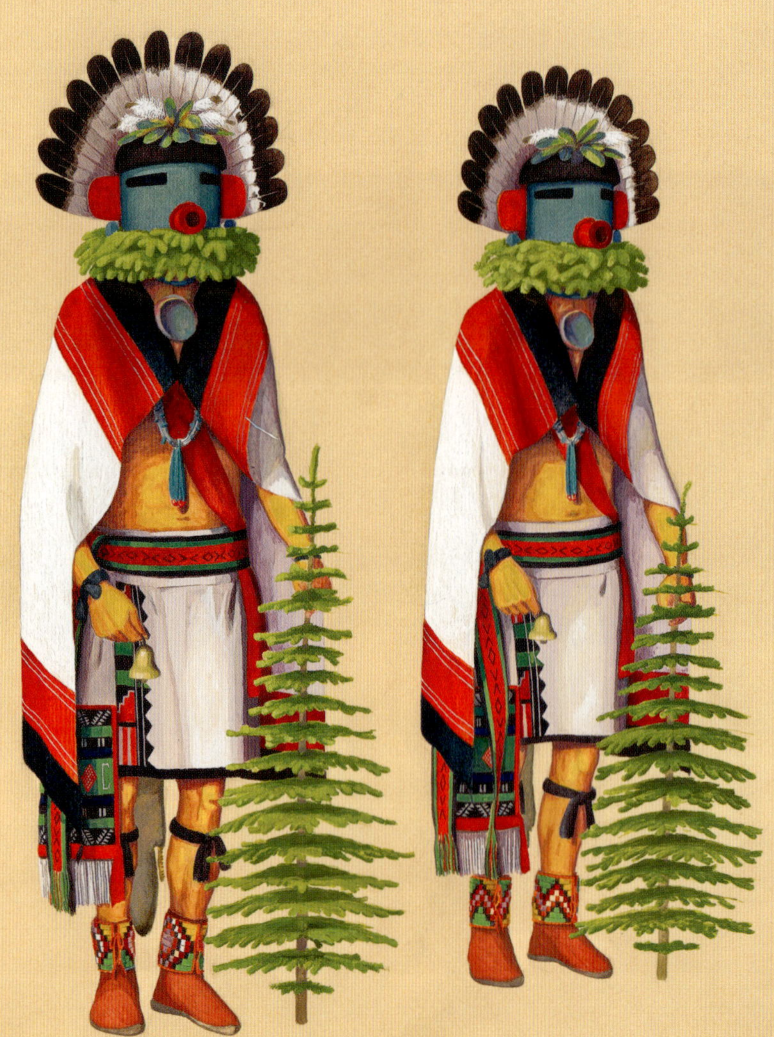
F. Kabotie

SEPTEMBER

Fred Kabotie
(Hopi Pueblo, 1900–1986)
Morning Kachinas, 1925–30
Watercolor on paper
14¾ × 11 in. (38 × 28 cm)
National Museum
of the American Indian

Raised on the Hopi Reservation in Shungopavi, Second Mesa, Arizona, Kabotie's Hopi name was Naqavoy'ma (Day After Day). Like most Hopi children at the time, he was required to attend a government-run school, Santa Fe Indian School, where he cultivated his artistic skills. He soon began selling his artworks and eventually became a preeminent silversmith, illustrator, potter, author, curator, and educator.

SUNDAY
5

LABOR DAY (US AND CAN.)

MONDAY
6

◐

TUESDAY
7

WEDNESDAY
8

THURSDAY
9

FRIDAY
10

SATURDAY
11

SEPTEMBER

S	M	T	W	T	F	S
			1	2	3	4
5	6	7	8	9	10	11
12	13	14	15	16	17	18
19	20	21	22	23	24	25
26	27	28	29	30		

OCTOBER

S	M	T	W	T	F	S
					1	2
3	4	5	6	7	8	9
10	11	12	13	14	15	16
17	18	19	20	21	22	23
24	25	26	27	28	29	30
31						

SEPTEMBER

SUNDAY

12

MONDAY

13

TUESDAY

14

WEDNESDAY ○

15

THURSDAY

16

FRIDAY

17

SATURDAY

18

Blue crab
(*Callinectes sapidus*)
7 × 7⅞ in. (17.6 × 20 cm)
National Museum
of Natural History

Native to the western Atlantic but introduced elsewhere, blue crabs play a vital economic role along the East Coast of the United States. In Maryland, the blue crab supports the state's largest commercial fishery and is the official state crustacean. Its blue tint comes from the interaction of alpha-crustacyanin and astaxanthin pigments in its shell.

SEPTEMBER

S	M	T	W	T	F	S
			1	2	3	4
5	6	7	8	9	10	11
12	13	14	15	16	17	18
19	20	21	22	23	24	25
26	27	28	29	30		

OCTOBER

S	M	T	W	T	F	S
					1	2
3	4	5	6	7	8	9
10	11	12	13	14	15	16
17	18	19	20	21	22	23
24	25	26	27	28	29	30
31						

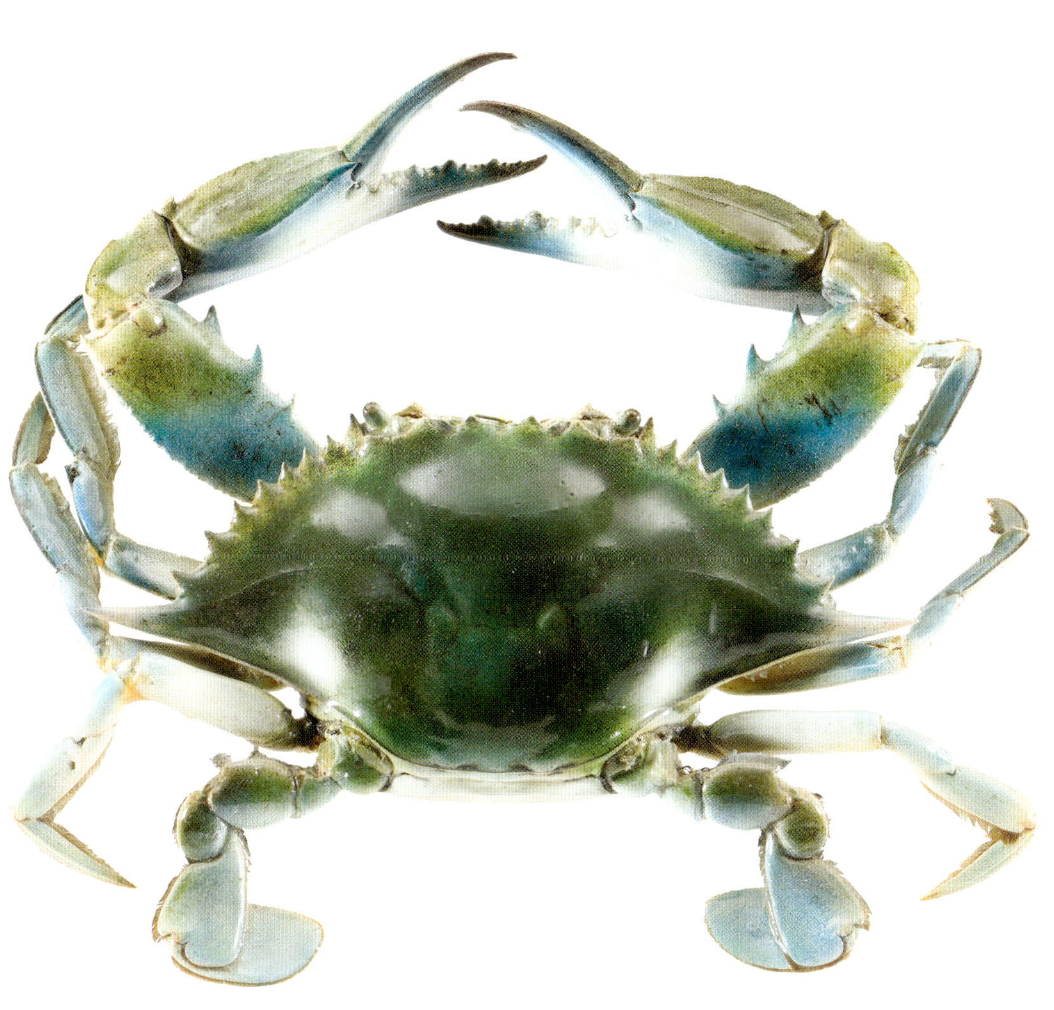

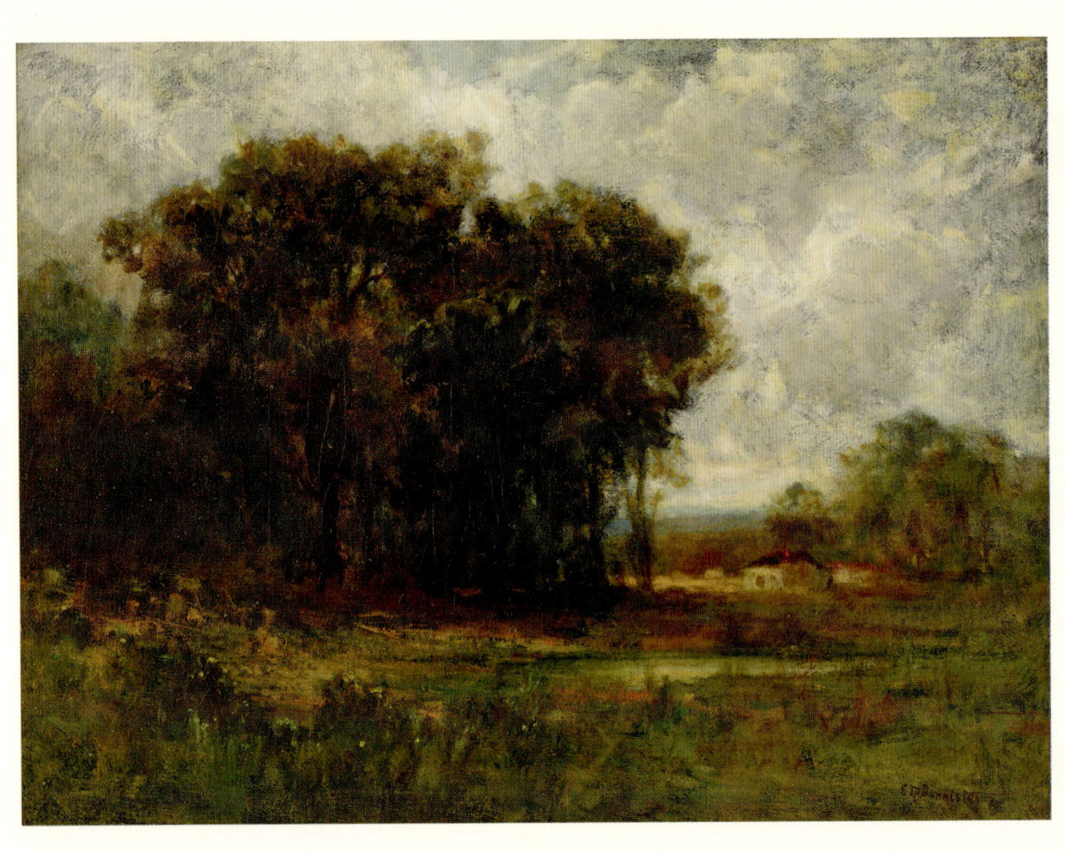

SEPTEMBER

Edward Mitchell Bannister (1828–1901)
At "Smith's Palace," Narragansett Bay, c. 1881
Oil on canvas
22 × 30 in. (60 × 76 cm)
National Museum of African American History and Culture

Edward Mitchell Bannister achieved financial success by painting portraits of the abolitionist community in Boston. After moving to Providence, Rhode Island, with his wife, Christiana Carteaux Bannister, he shifted his focus to landscapes. A leader of the local arts community, Bannister was a founding member of the Rhode Island School of Design and the Providence Art Club.

SUNDAY

19

MONDAY

20

TUESDAY

21

WEDNESDAY

22

◑ FIRST DAY OF AUTUMN

THURSDAY

23

FRIDAY

24

SATURDAY

25

SEPTEMBER

S	M	T	W	T	F	S
			1	2	3	4
5	6	7	8	9	10	11
12	13	14	15	16	17	18
19	20	21	22	23	24	25
26	27	28	29	30		

OCTOBER

S	M	T	W	T	F	S
					1	2
3	4	5	6	7	8	9
10	11	12	13	14	15	16
17	18	19	20	21	22	23
24	25	26	27	28	29	30
31						

SEPTEMBER · OCTOBER

SUNDAY

26

MONDAY

27

TUESDAY

28

WEDNESDAY ●

29

THURSDAY

30

FRIDAY ROSH HASHANAH BEGINS (SUNDOWN)

1

SATURDAY

2

Alma Thomas (1891–1978)
Aquatic Gardens, 1973
Acrylic on canvas
72 × 52 in. (183 × 132 cm)
Smithsonian American Art Museum

Aquatic Gardens may have been inspired by a visit to Kenilworth Park and Aquatic Gardens, a national park in Washington, DC, devoted to the cultivation of water plants. Thomas did not paint outdoors, considering this to be an old-fashioned approach. She instead sought out sensory experiences in person that she later translated into painting in her studio.

SEPTEMBER

S	M	T	W	T	F	S
			1	2	3	4
5	6	7	8	9	10	11
12	13	14	15	16	17	18
19	20	21	22	23	24	25
26	27	28	29	30		

OCTOBER

S	M	T	W	T	F	S
					1	2
3	4	5	6	7	8	9
10	11	12	13	14	15	16
17	18	19	20	21	22	23
24	25	26	27	28	29	30
31						

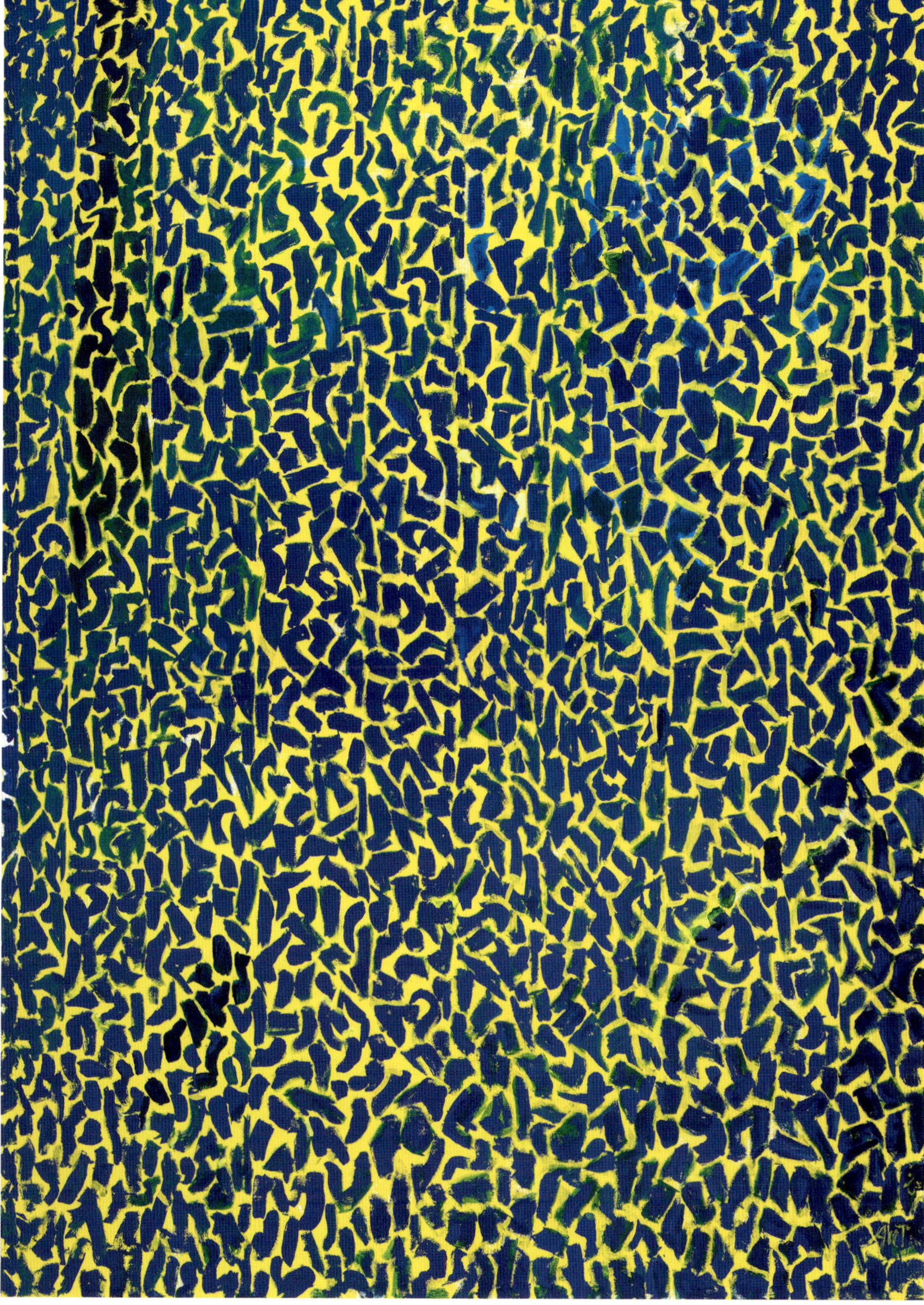

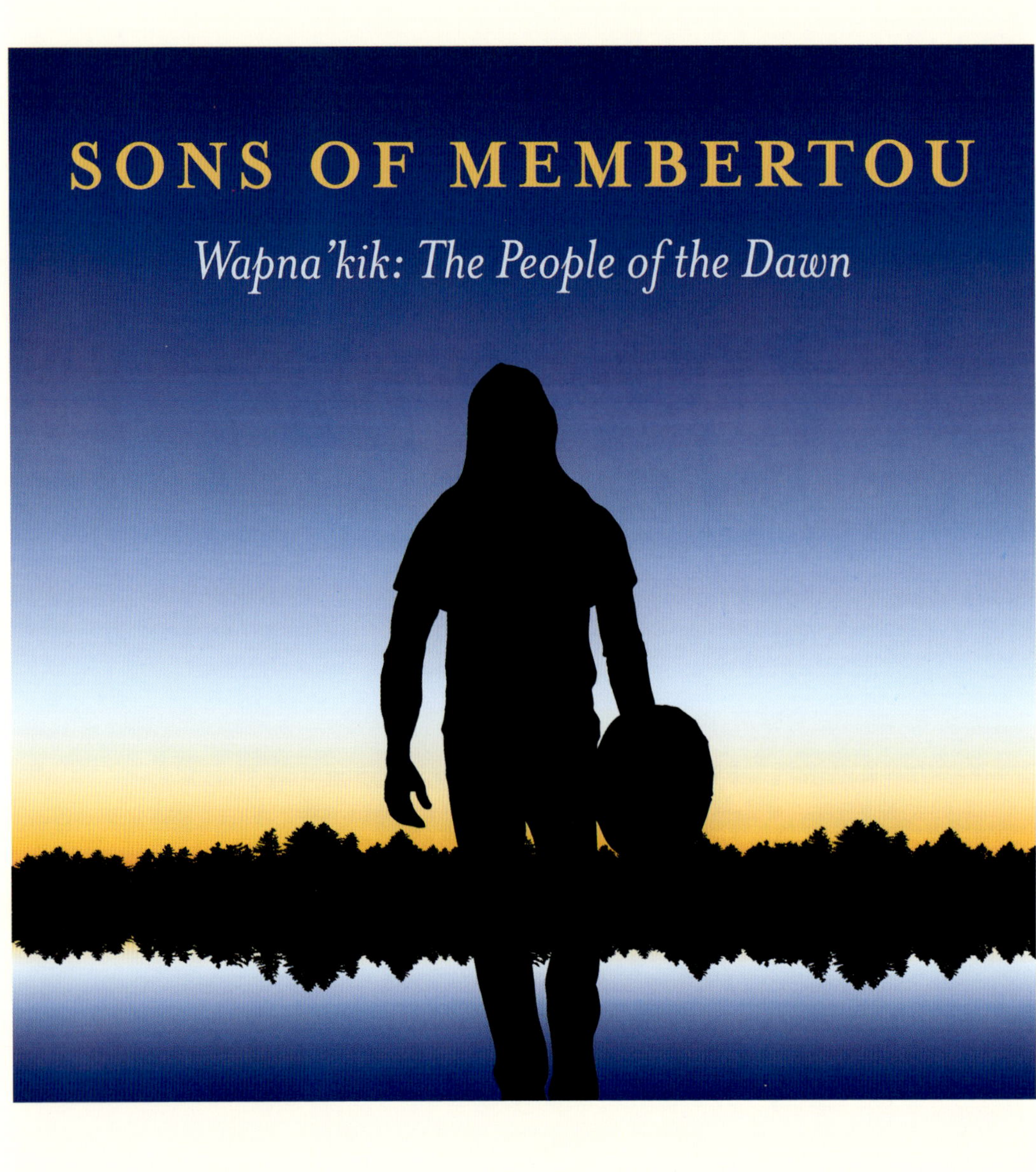
SONS OF MEMBERTOU
Wapna'kik: The People of the Dawn

OCTOBER

Wapna'kik: The People of the Dawn, 2025
Sons of Membertou
Cover artwork by Gerald Richard Gloade
Cover design by Cooley Design Lab
4¾ × 4¾ in. (12 × 12 cm)
Smithsonian Folkways Recordings

Wapna'kik: The People of the Dawn by the musical group Sons of Membertou foregrounds the powerful voices of the Mi'kmaw people. First released in 1995, *Wapna'kik* documents a vital resurgence of the Membertou community's music practices. This updated edition includes "Kepmite'tmnej (Mi'kmaq Honour Song)" and "500 Years," introducing a new generation of singers and musicians.

ROSH HASHANAH ENDS (SUNDOWN)

SUNDAY
3

MONDAY
4

TUESDAY
5

WEDNESDAY
6

◐

THURSDAY
7

FRIDAY
8

SATURDAY
9

OCTOBER

S	M	T	W	T	F	S
					1	2
3	4	5	6	7	8	9
10	11	12	13	14	15	16
17	18	19	20	21	22	23
24	25	26	27	28	29	30
31						

NOVEMBER

S	M	T	W	T	F	S
	1	2	3	4	5	6
7	8	9	10	11	12	13
14	15	16	17	18	19	20
21	22	23	24	25	26	27
28	29	30				

OCTOBER

SUNDAY

YOM KIPPUR BEGINS (SUNDOWN)

10

MONDAY

COLUMBUS DAY/INDIGENOUS PEOPLES' DAY (US)

THANKSGIVING DAY (CAN.)

YOM KIPPUR ENDS (SUNDOWN)

11

TUESDAY

12

WEDNESDAY

13

THURSDAY

14

FRIDAY

○

15

SATURDAY

16

4¢ Forest Conservation stamp, 1958
Paper, ink, adhesive
1⁹⁄₁₆ × 1 in. (4 × 2.5 cm)
National Postal Museum

In addition to publicizing forest conservation, this stamp was issued in commemoration of the 100th anniversary of the birth of Theodore Roosevelt, the 26th US president. Roosevelt was one of the first American leaders to promote the need to preserve and protect the nation's natural resources.

OCTOBER

S	M	T	W	T	F	S
					1	2
3	4	5	6	7	8	9
10	11	12	13	14	15	16
17	18	19	20	21	22	23
24	25	26	27	28	29	30
31						

NOVEMBER

S	M	T	W	T	F	S
	1	2	3	4	5	6
7	8	9	10	11	12	13
14	15	16	17	18	19	20
21	22	23	24	25	26	27
28	29	30				

FOREST CONSERVATION

U.S. POSTAGE 4¢

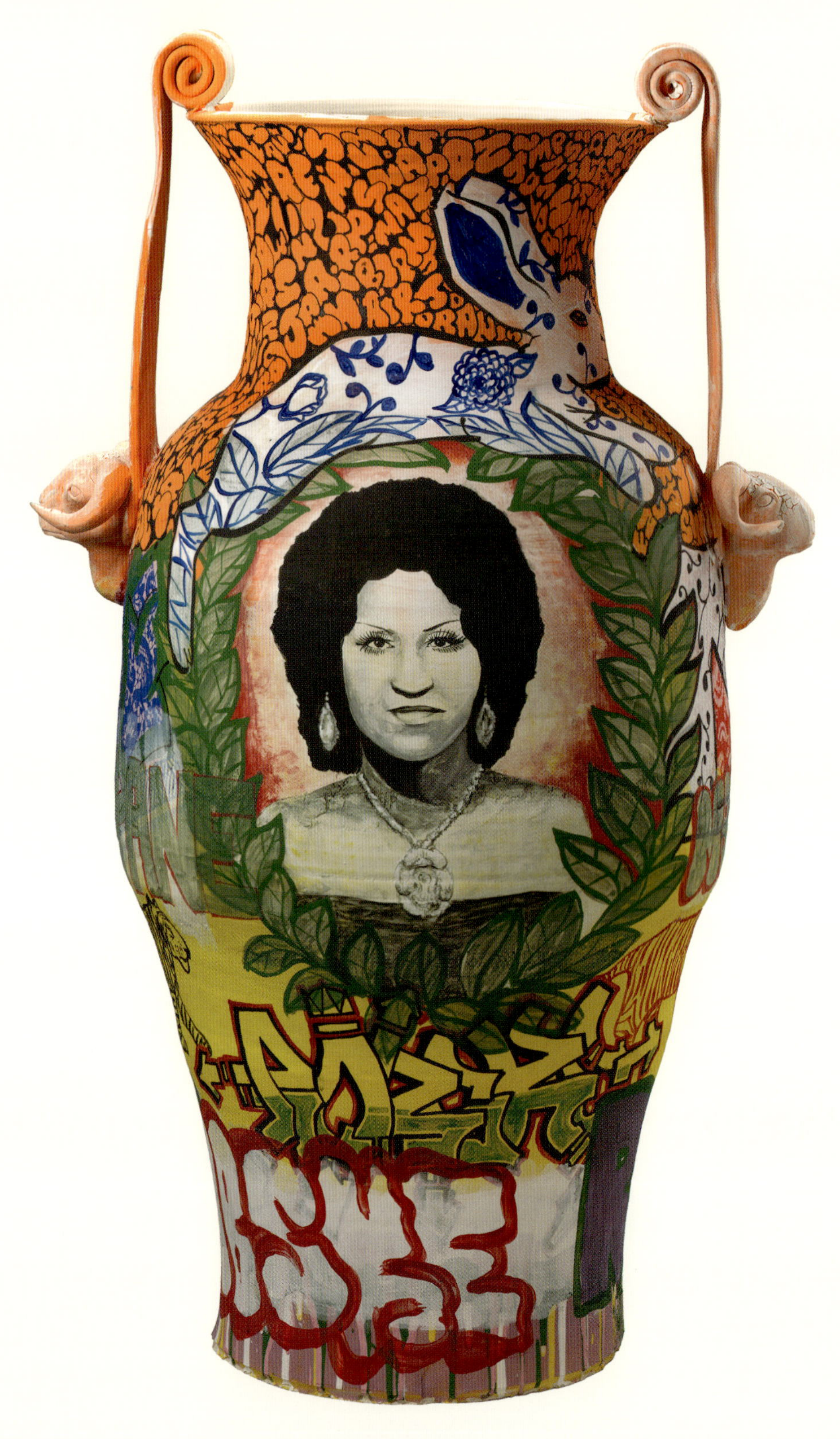

Smithsonian Books publishes works based on museums, collections, and artifacts, as well as on topics where the Smithsonian's authority is unparalleled, such as history; natural history; science and technology; space; aviation, and military; and art.

Smithsonian Books titles are available for purchase wherever books are sold. You may also place your order directly from the Smithsonian by calling 1-800-322-0344 or visiting SmithsonianStore.com.

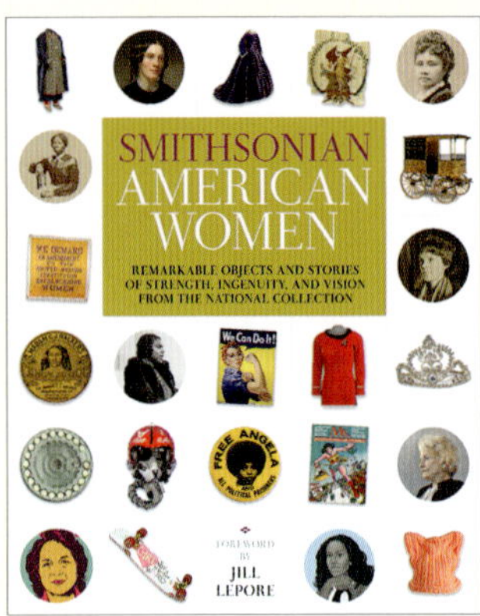

Smithsonian American Women, $40.00, 248 pages, 9 × 11 in.; 9781588346650

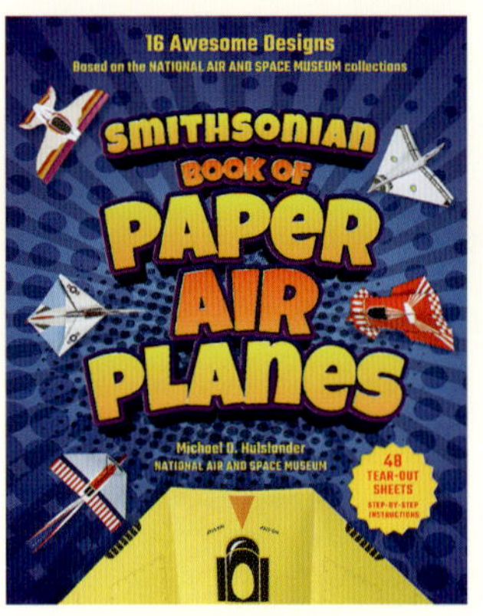

Smithsonian Book of Paper Airplanes, $16.95, 224 pages, $8\frac{1}{2} \times 10\frac{3}{16}$ in.; 9781588347787

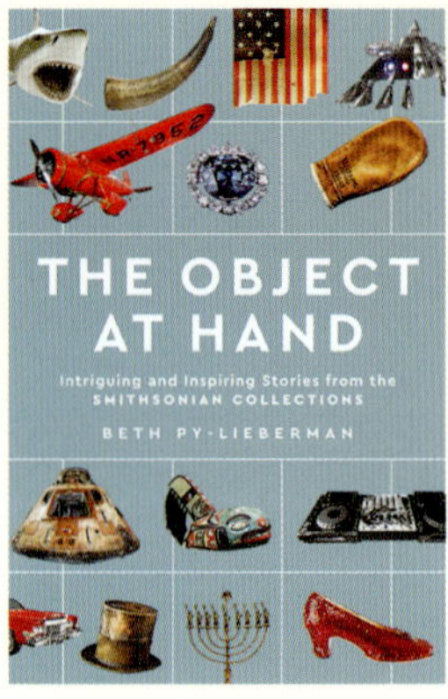

The Object at Hand, Beth Py-Lieberman, $29.95, 304 pages, 6 × 9 in.; 9781588347497

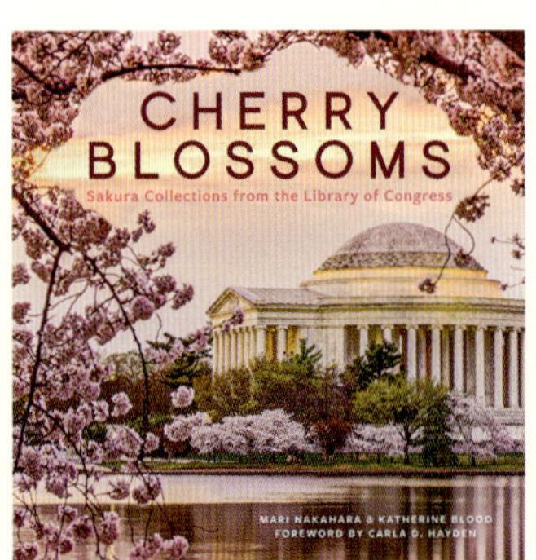

Cherry Blossoms, Mari Nakahara and Katherine Blood, $18.95, 96 pages, 8 × 8 in.; 9781588346841

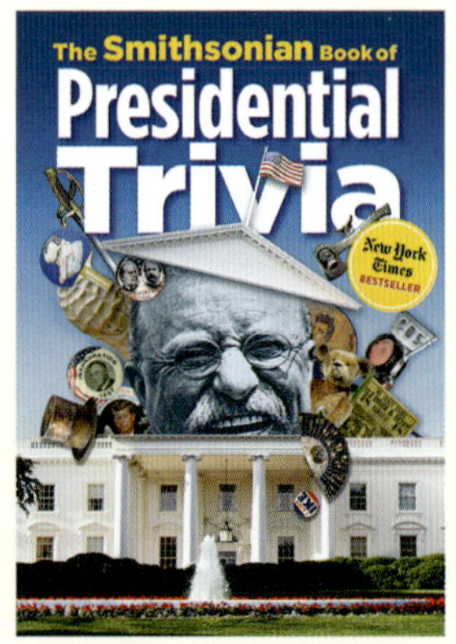

The Smithsonian Book of Presidential Trivia, $12.95, 240 pages, 6 × 8 in.; 9781588343253

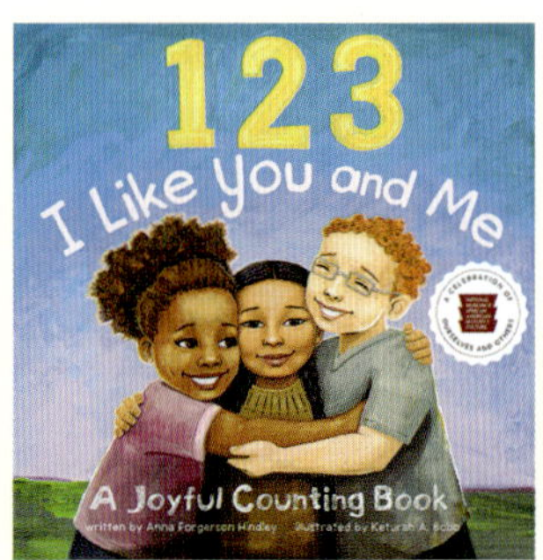

123 I Like You and Me, $9.95, 224 pages, 6 × 6 in.; 9781588347961

For a full list of Smithsonian Books titles, go to smithsonianbooks.com.

OCTOBER

Roberto Lugo (b. 1981)
Celia Cruz, 2022
Ceramic
37⅜ × 23 × 17 in.
(95 × 58.5 × 43 cm)
Museum purchase through the Smithsonian Latino Initiatives Pool, administered by the National Museum of the American Latino
National Portrait Gallery

With her powerful voice, Celia Cruz (1925–2003) fused Puerto Rican and Cuban rhythms in 1970s New York. The ceramicist Roberto Lugo shaped this vase like a Greek amphora and imbued it with the aesthetics of hip-hop to honor the timeless "Queen of Salsa."

SUNDAY
17

MONDAY
18

TUESDAY
19

WEDNESDAY
20

THURSDAY
21

◑

FRIDAY
22

SATURDAY
23

OCTOBER

S	M	T	W	T	F	S
					1	2
3	4	5	6	7	8	9
10	11	12	13	14	15	16
17	18	19	20	21	22	23
24	25	26	27	28	29	30
31						

NOVEMBER

S	M	T	W	T	F	S
	1	2	3	4	5	6
7	8	9	10	11	12	13
14	15	16	17	18	19	20
21	22	23	24	25	26	27
28	29	30				

OCTOBER

SUNDAY

24

MONDAY

25

TUESDAY

26

WEDNESDAY

27

THURSDAY

28

FRIDAY

29

SATURDAY

30

Miniature topeng
Java, Indonesia
Paint, wood
2½ × 2⅛ × 1⁵⁄₁₆ in.
(6.5 × 5.5 × 3.3 cm)
National Museum
of Natural History

This miniature topeng, or mask, was collected in Java by Ann Dunham, an anthropologist whose work focused on rural development, economics, and women's rights in Indonesia. She was also the mother of Barack Obama, the 44th president of the United States. Life-size topeng are worn in traditional Indonesian dance performances.

OCTOBER

S	M	T	W	T	F	S
					1	2
3	4	5	6	7	8	9
10	11	12	13	14	15	16
17	18	19	20	21	22	23
24	25	26	27	28	29	30
31						

NOVEMBER

S	M	T	W	T	F	S
	1	2	3	4	5	6
7	8	9	10	11	12	13
14	15	16	17	18	19	20
21	22	23	24	25	26	27
28	29	30				

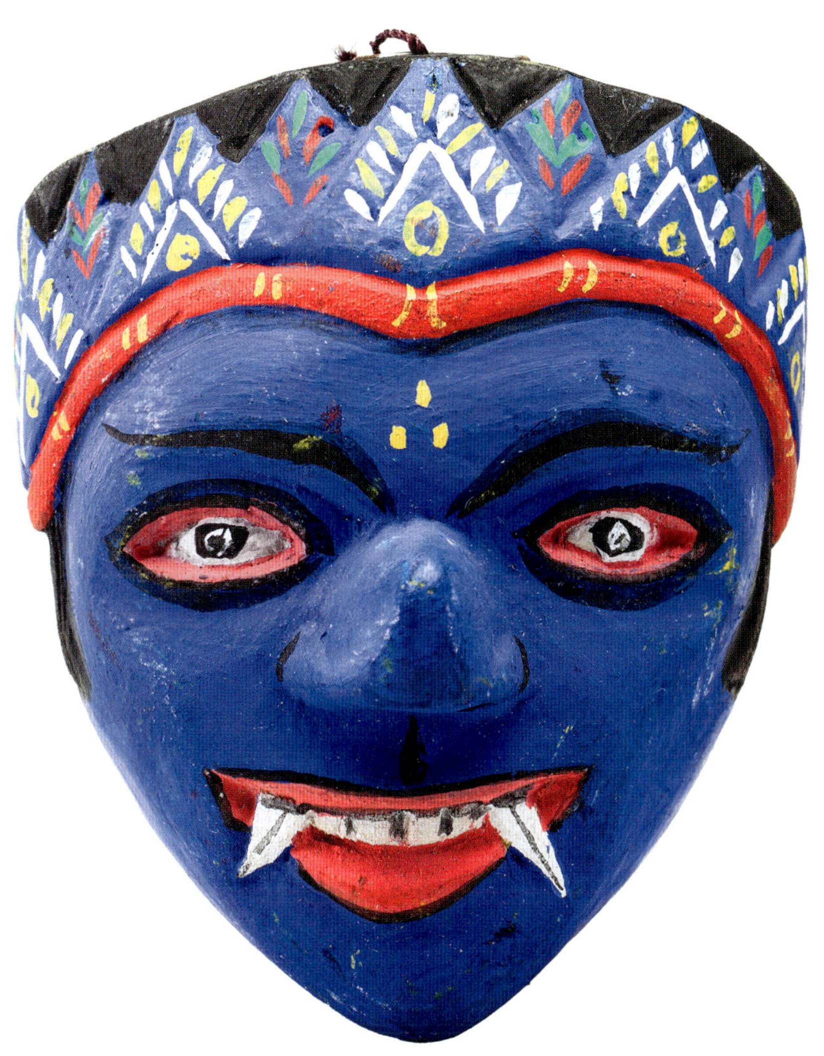

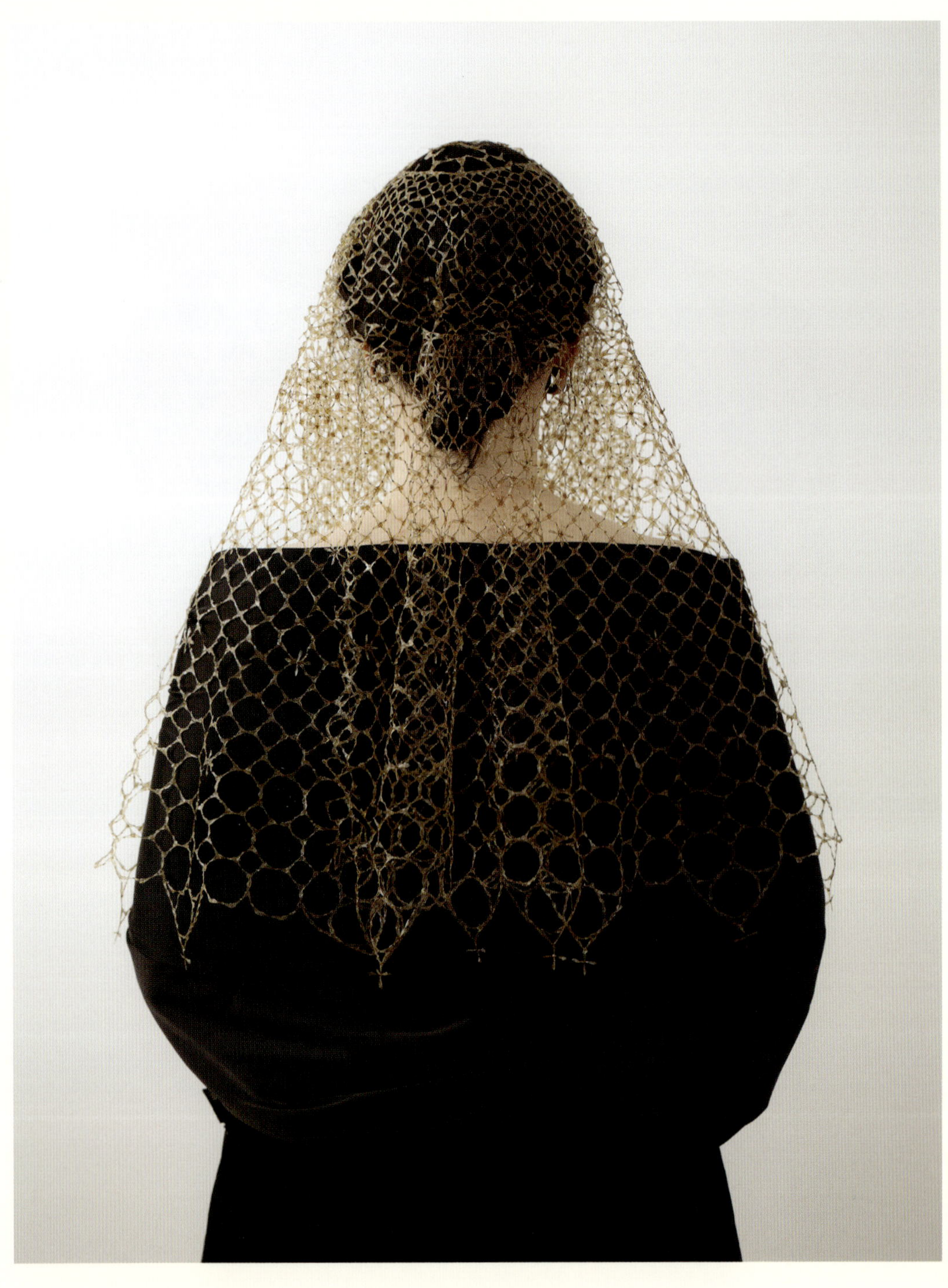

Luci Jockel (b. 1991)
Gold Veil, 2023
Honeybee wings, archival glue
Diameter: 49 in. (124.5 cm)
Smithsonian American Art Museum

Luci Jockel's *Gold Veil* is an homage to the communal labor and ephemeral life of the bee. It is constructed from more than 20,000 wings of desiccated honeybees, which the artist found while assisting beekeepers in rebuilding their hives. The "bee wing lace" pattern of this veil references Victorian mourning attire and stained-glass cathedral windows.

HALLOWEEN

SUNDAY
31

MONDAY
1

ELECTION DAY (US)

TUESDAY
2

WEDNESDAY
3

THURSDAY
4

FRIDAY
5

◐

SATURDAY
6

OCTOBER

S	M	T	W	T	F	S
					1	2
3	4	5	6	7	8	9
10	11	12	13	14	15	16
17	18	19	20	21	22	23
24	25	26	27	28	29	30
31						

NOVEMBER

S	M	T	W	T	F	S
	1	2	3	4	5	6
7	8	9	10	11	12	13
14	15	16	17	18	19	20
21	22	23	24	25	26	27
28	29	30				

NOVEMBER

SUNDAY

7

DAYLIGHT SAVING TIME ENDS

MONDAY

8

TUESDAY

9

WEDNESDAY

10

THURSDAY

11

VETERANS DAY (US)

REMEMBRANCE DAY (CAN.)

FRIDAY

12

SATURDAY

13

○

Luis Rosa-Valentín
(b. 1983)
Self-Portrait in Uniform, 2021
Oil on canvas
28 × 22 in. (71 × 56 cm)
National Museum
of the American Latino

In this self-portrait, Luis Rosa-Valentín wears his army dress uniform with military honors prominently featured. His injuries, the result of an improvised explosive device in Iraq, are intentionally displayed: Seated in his wheelchair, his prosthetic arm, amputations, and cochlear implant are visible. Rosa-Valentín began painting during his rehabilitation and later earned a degree in fine arts.

NOVEMBER

S	M	T	W	T	F	S
	1	2	3	4	5	6
7	8	9	10	11	12	13
14	15	16	17	18	19	20
21	22	23	24	25	26	27
28	29	30				

DECEMBER

S	M	T	W	T	F	S
			1	2	3	4
5	6	7	8	9	10	11
12	13	14	15	16	17	18
19	20	21	22	23	24	25
26	27	28	29	30	31	

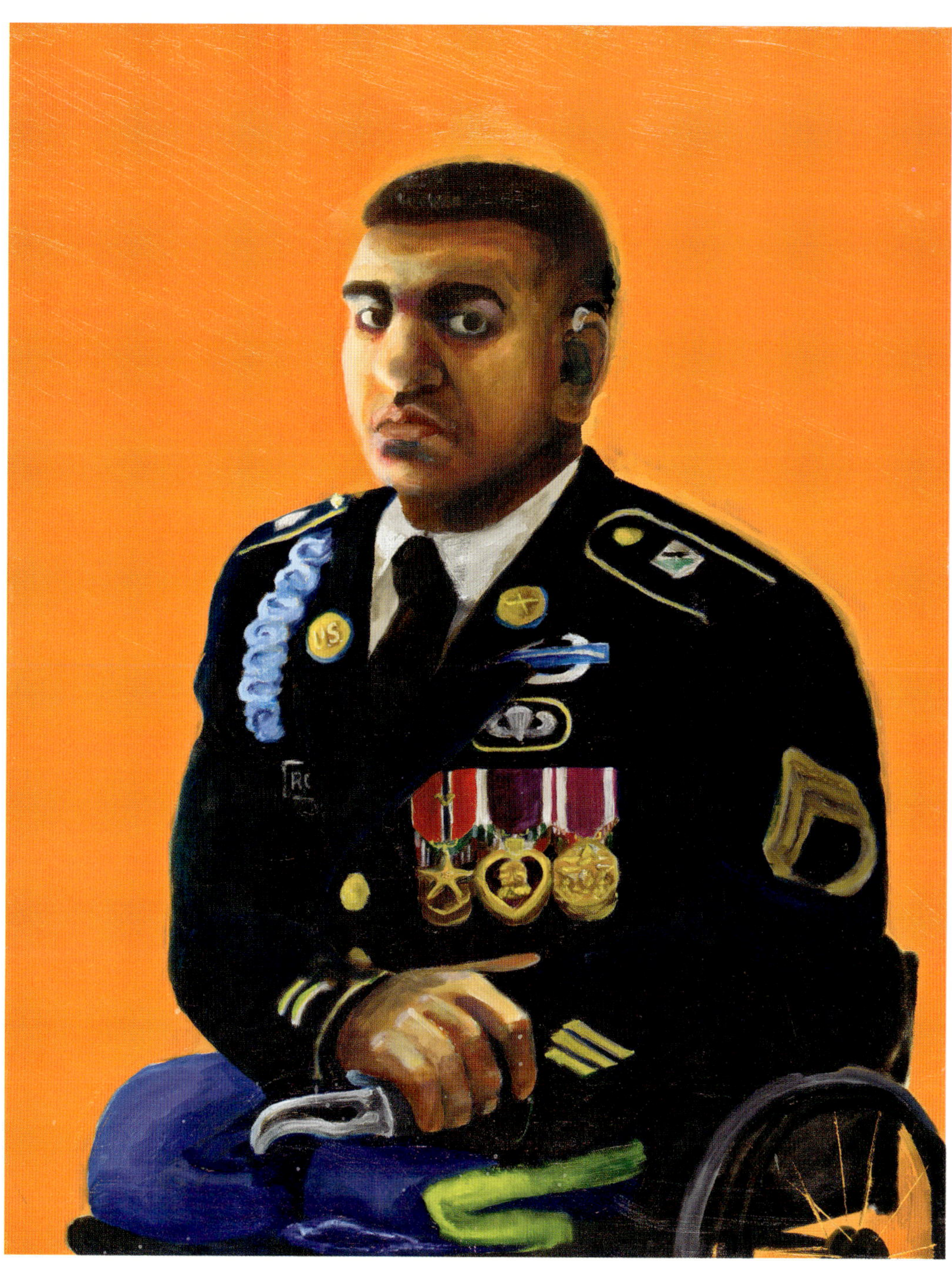
US

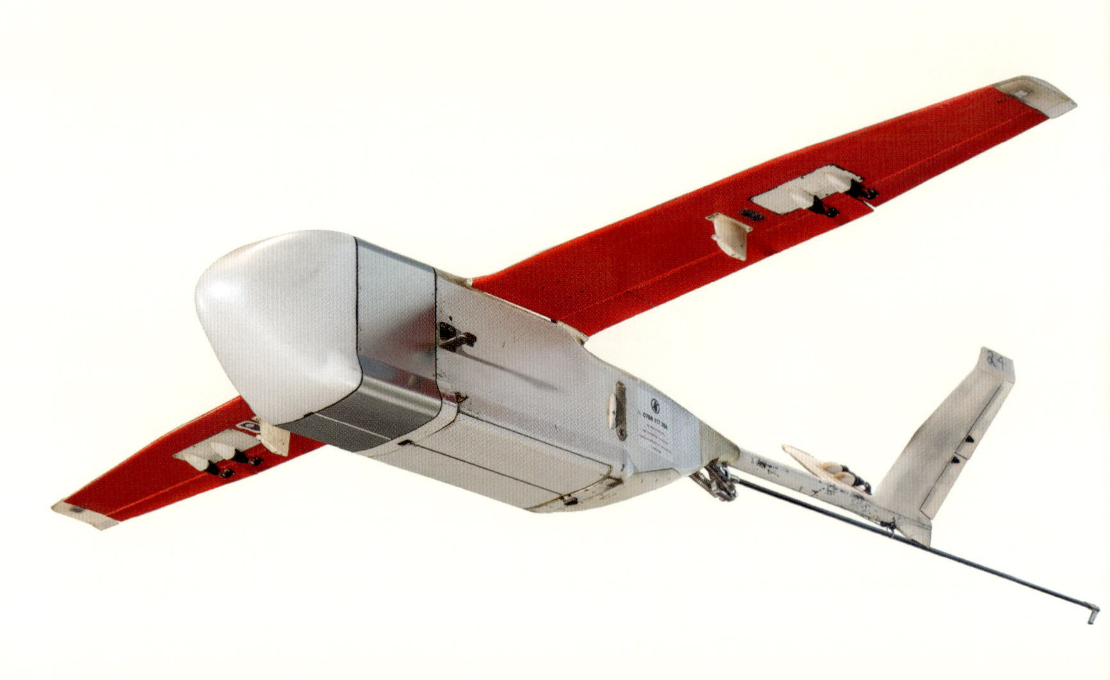

NOVEMBER

Delivery drone, 2016
Zipline International Inc.,
South San Francisco, CA
7 ft. 2½ in. × 1 ft. 4¾ in. × 7 ft. ½ in.
(219.7 × 42.5 × 214.6 cm)
National Air and Space Museum

Red and white drones like this one made by the American company Zipline are used to deliver blood and other medical supplies to hospitals and clinics domestically and in foreign countries such as Rwanda, Ghana, and Japan. Drone deliveries are able to take direct paths rather than winding roads in rural and other areas, reducing wait times for critical supplies.

SUNDAY 14

MONDAY 15

TUESDAY 16

WEDNESDAY 17

THURSDAY 18

FRIDAY 19

◑ SATURDAY 20

NOVEMBER

S	M	T	W	T	F	S
	1	2	3	4	5	6
7	8	9	10	11	12	13
14	15	16	17	18	19	20
21	22	23	24	25	26	27
28	29	30				

DECEMBER

S	M	T	W	T	F	S
			1	2	3	4
5	6	7	8	9	10	11
12	13	14	15	16	17	18
19	20	21	22	23	24	25
26	27	28	29	30	31	

NOVEMBER

SUNDAY

21

MONDAY

22

TUESDAY

23

WEDNESDAY

24

THURSDAY

THANKSGIVING DAY (US)

25

FRIDAY

26

SATURDAY

27

Lucy Bull (b. 1990)
12:18, 2022
Oil on linen
60 × 30¼ × 1⅝ in.
(152.4 × 76.8 × 4.1 cm)
Gift of Iris and
Adam Singer
Hirshhorn Museum
and Sculpture Garden

Lucy Bull creates large-scale abstract paintings in acidic color palettes that have earned her comparisons to early twentieth-century Fauvist painters such as Henri Matisse. Bull employs these vivid hues to stimulate a visceral, transcendent engagement with painting that fosters sensations like awe and wonder as the intellect surrenders to the imagination.

NOVEMBER

S	M	T	W	T	F	S
	1	2	3	4	5	6
7	8	9	10	11	12	13
14	15	16	17	18	19	20
21	22	23	24	25	26	27
28	29	30				

DECEMBER

S	M	T	W	T	F	S
			1	2	3	4
5	6	7	8	9	10	11
12	13	14	15	16	17	18
19	20	21	22	23	24	25
26	27	28	29	30	31	

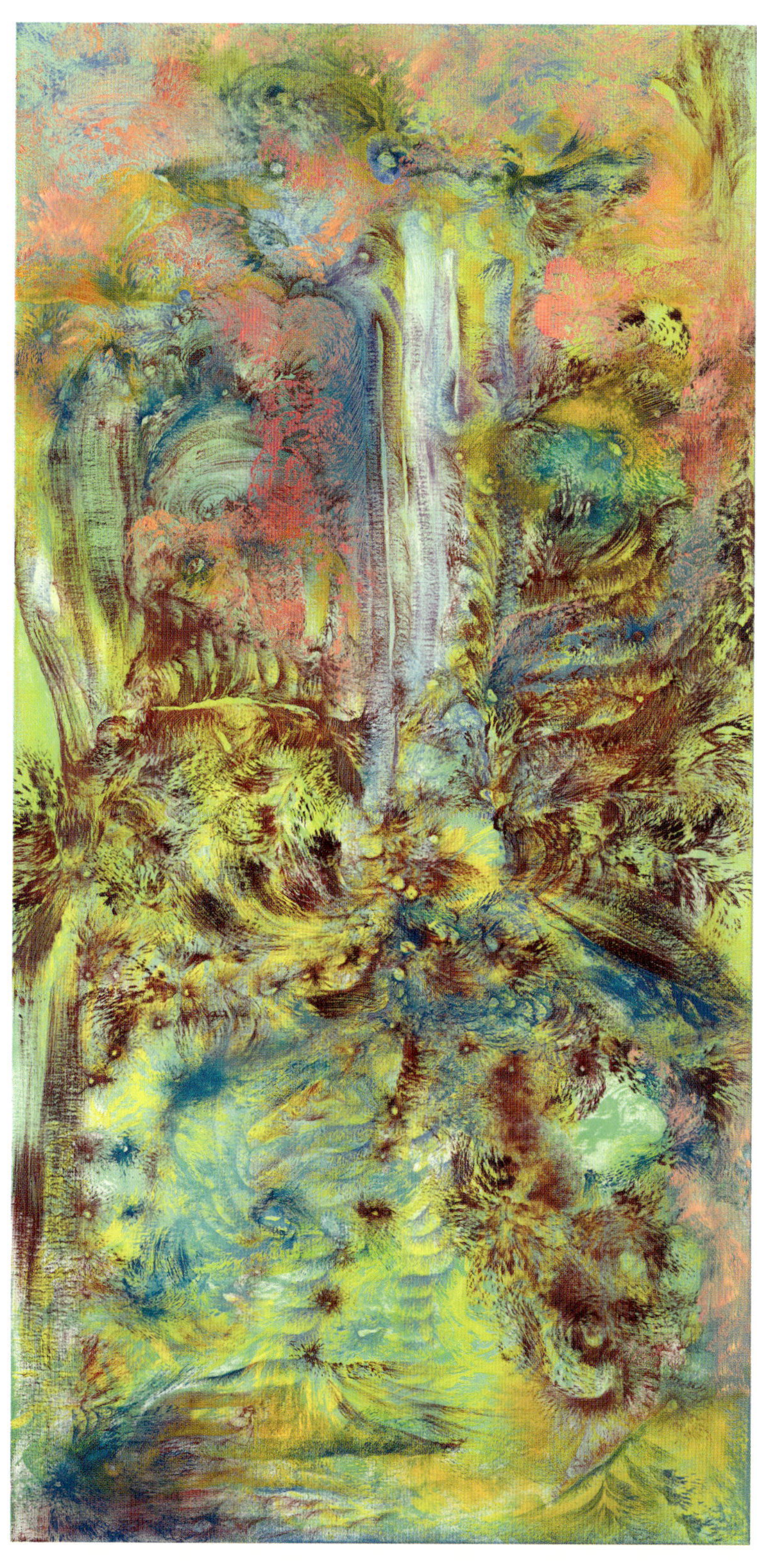

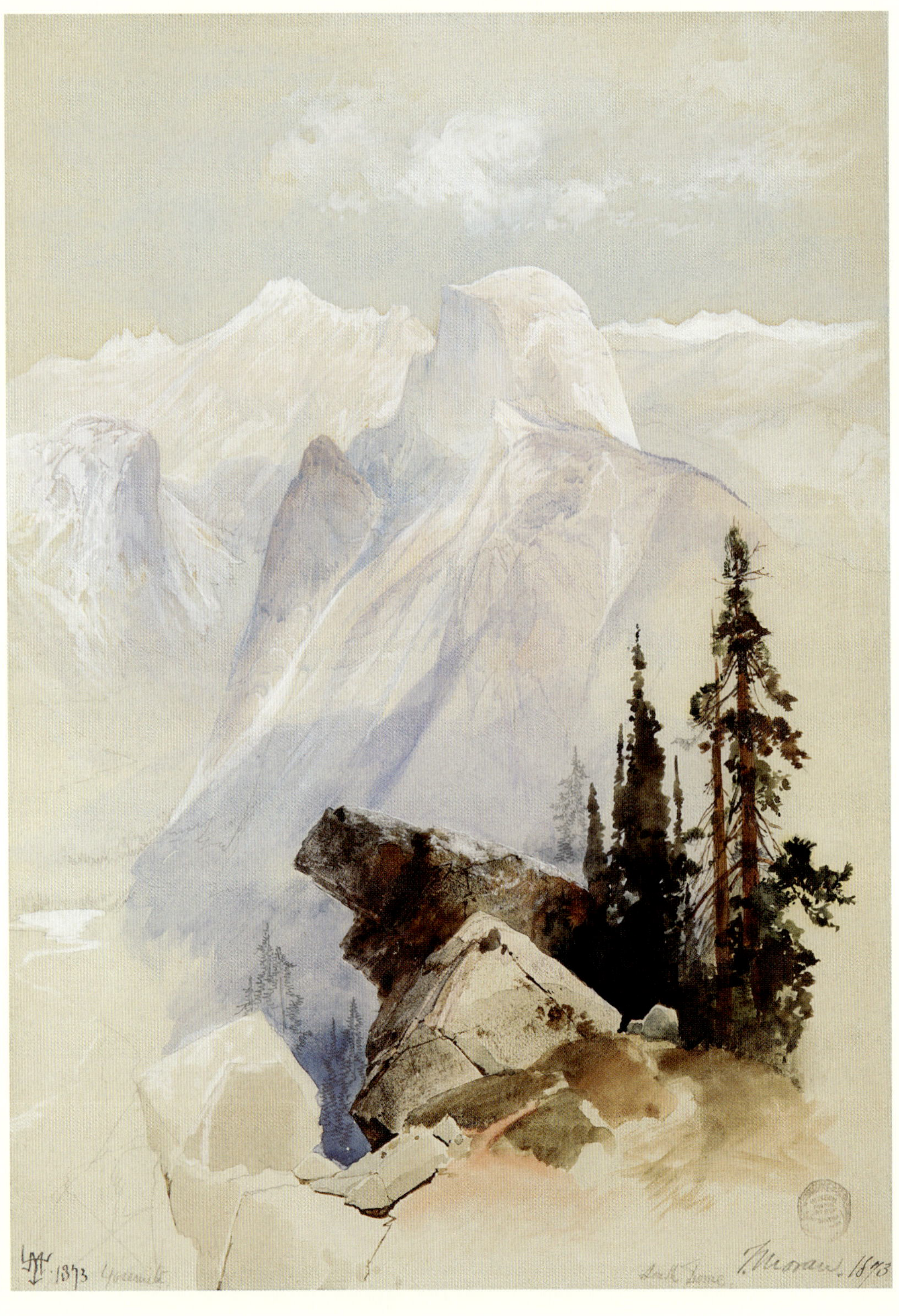

NOVEMBER · DECEMBER

Thomas Moran
(1837–1926)
Half Dome, Yosemite, 1873
Watercolor, white gouache, graphite on blue-gray wove paper
14½ × 10⅛ in.
(36.9 × 25.7 cm)
Gift of Thomas Moran
Cooper Hewitt, Smithsonian Design Museum

Moran visited Yosemite in August 1872. This drawing of the view from Glacier Point looking up the canyon was completed a year later from sketches done in the field and from published photographic sources. Moran's opalescent view of this natural wonder conveys the thin atmosphere and the shimmering effects of light.

NOVEMBER

S	M	T	W	T	F	S
	1	2	3	4	5	6
7	8	9	10	11	12	13
14	15	16	17	18	19	20
21	22	23	24	25	26	27
28	29	30				

DECEMBER

S	M	T	W	T	F	S
			1	2	3	4
5	6	7	8	9	10	11
12	13	14	15	16	17	18
19	20	21	22	23	24	25
26	27	28	29	30	31	

SUNDAY

28

MONDAY

29

TUESDAY

30

WEDNESDAY

1

THURSDAY

2

FRIDAY

3

SATURDAY

4

DECEMBER

SUNDAY

5

MONDAY ◐

6

TUESDAY

7

WEDNESDAY

8

THURSDAY

9

FRIDAY HUMAN RIGHTS DAY

10

SATURDAY

11

Gordon Parks (1912–2006)
Washington, D.C. Government Charwoman (American Gothic), 1942
Silver gelatin print
14 × 11 in. (35.5 × 28 cm)
National Museum of African American History and Culture

As a photographer for the Farm Security Administration, Gordon Parks documented the joys and struggles of African Americans in Washington, DC. The resulting photographs offered a perspective on life beyond the facade of the capital city. Ella Watson, pictured here, allowed Parks access to her home life, caring for her grandchildren, and her work life, cleaning government offices.

DECEMBER

S	M	T	W	T	F	S
			1	2	3	4
5	6	7	8	9	10	11
12	13	14	15	16	17	18
19	20	21	22	23	24	25
26	27	28	29	30	31	

JANUARY 2028

S	M	T	W	T	F	S
						1
2	3	4	5	6	7	8
9	10	11	12	13	14	15
16	17	18	19	20	21	22
23	24	25	26	27	28	29
30	31					

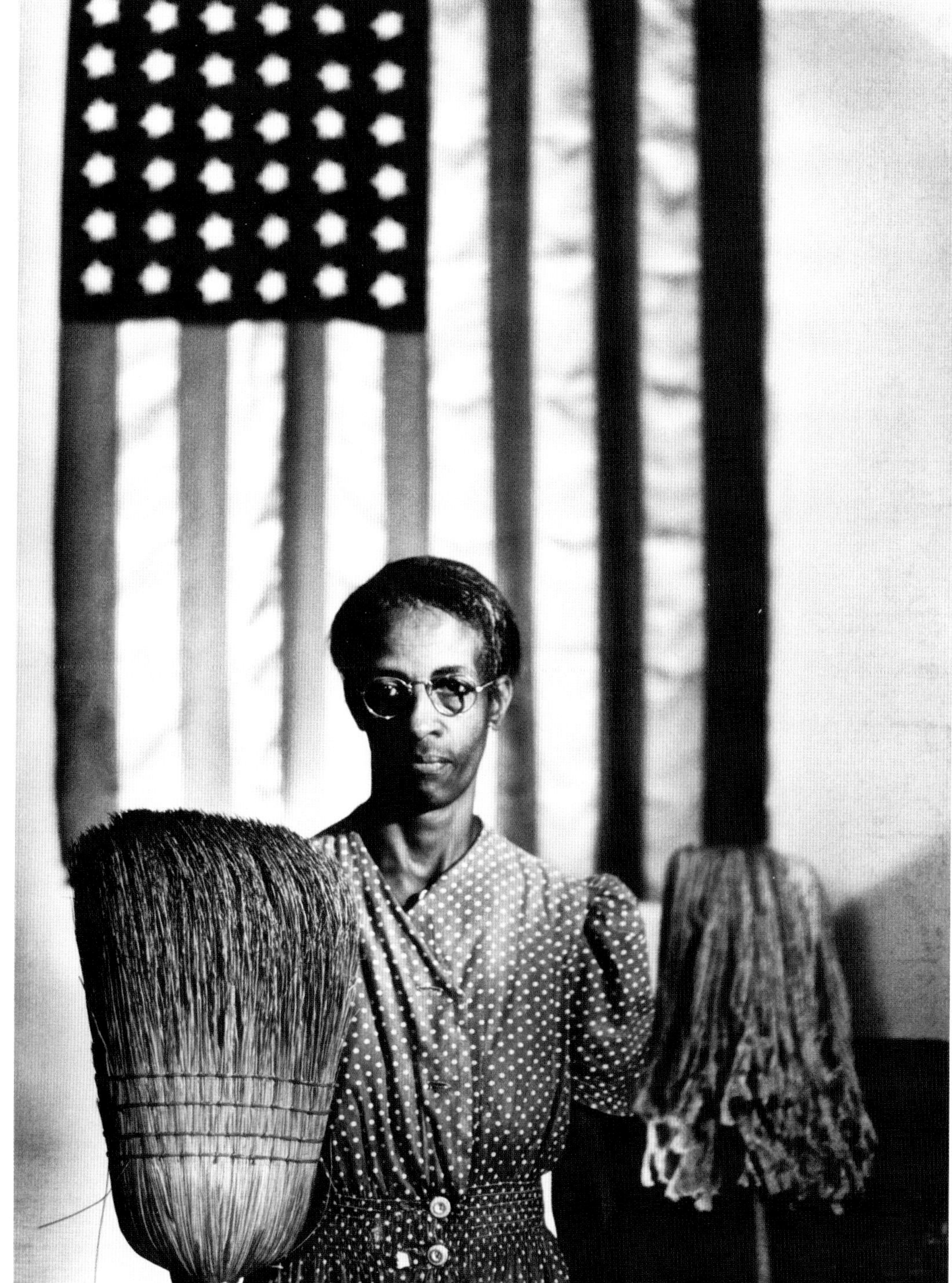

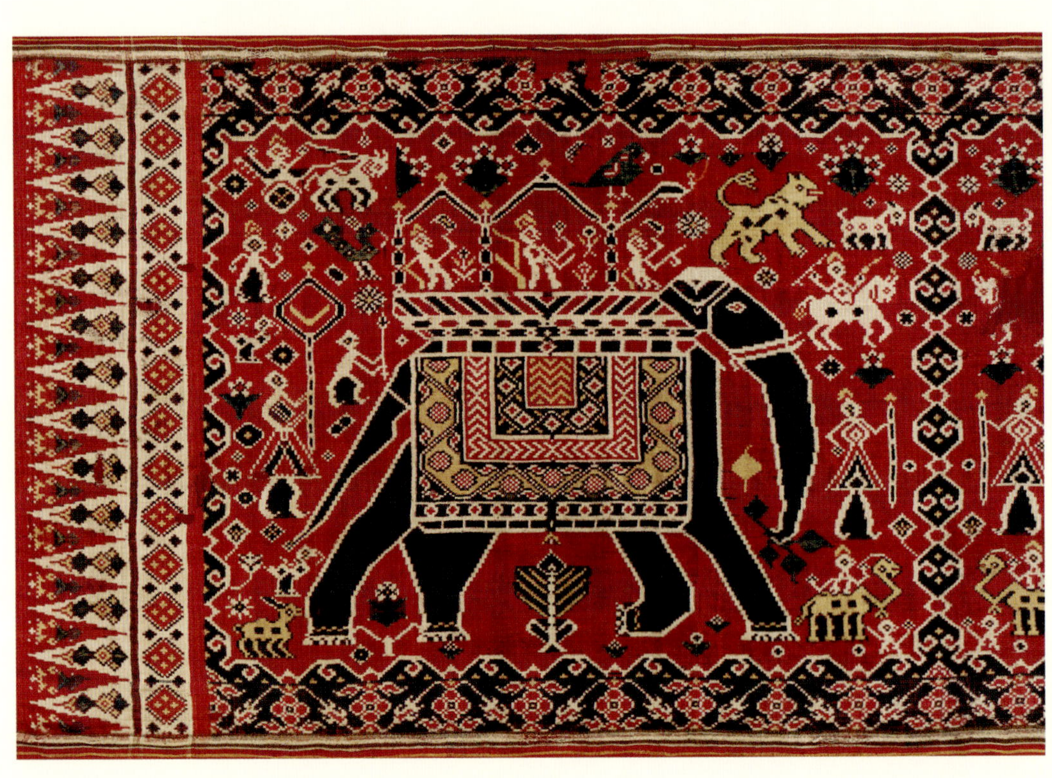

DECEMBER

Detail from a ceremonial double ikat (*patolu*): Elephants in a royal hunt, 17th–18th century
Gujarat state, India
Silk
44 × 192 in. (112 × 488 cm)
National Museum of Asian Art

Elephants embark on a grand procession through an enchanted forest in this complex sixteen-foot-wide textile. Works such as this, woven in Gujarat from deeply saturated and rarely produced silks, were among the most important Indian exports to Southeast Asia.

SUNDAY
12

○
MONDAY
13

TUESDAY
14

WEDNESDAY
15

THURSDAY
16

FRIDAY
17

SATURDAY
18

DECEMBER

S	M	T	W	T	F	S
			1	2	3	4
5	6	7	8	9	10	11
12	13	14	15	16	17	18
19	20	21	22	23	24	25
26	27	28	29	30	31	

JANUARY 2028

S	M	T	W	T	F	S
						1
2	3	4	5	6	7	8
9	10	11	12	13	14	15
16	17	18	19	20	21	22
23	24	25	26	27	28	29
30	31					

DECEMBER

SUNDAY

19

MONDAY ◑

20

TUESDAY FIRST DAY OF WINTER

21

WEDNESDAY

22

THURSDAY

23

FRIDAY CHRISTMAS EVE

HANUKKAH BEGINS (SUNDOWN)

24

SATURDAY CHRISTMAS

25

Julia Thecla (1896–1973)
Christmas card to Katharine Kuh, c. 1960s
Oil, ink, various other media on cardstock
6¼ × 4⅜ in. (16 × 11 cm)
Katharine Kuh papers, 1875–1994
Archives of American Art

Thecla was a watercolorist living in Chicago known for her dazzling surrealist compositions. Katharine Kuh was a major Chicago art dealer and curator who brought the avant-garde to a ready public. A sliver of Midwestern winter glistens through this holiday card by the artist.

DECEMBER

S	M	T	W	T	F	S
			1	2	3	4
5	6	7	8	9	10	11
12	13	14	15	16	17	18
19	20	21	22	23	24	25
26	27	28	29	30	31	

JANUARY 2028

S	M	T	W	T	F	S
						1
2	3	4	5	6	7	8
9	10	11	12	13	14	15
16	17	18	19	20	21	22
23	24	25	26	27	28	29
30	31					

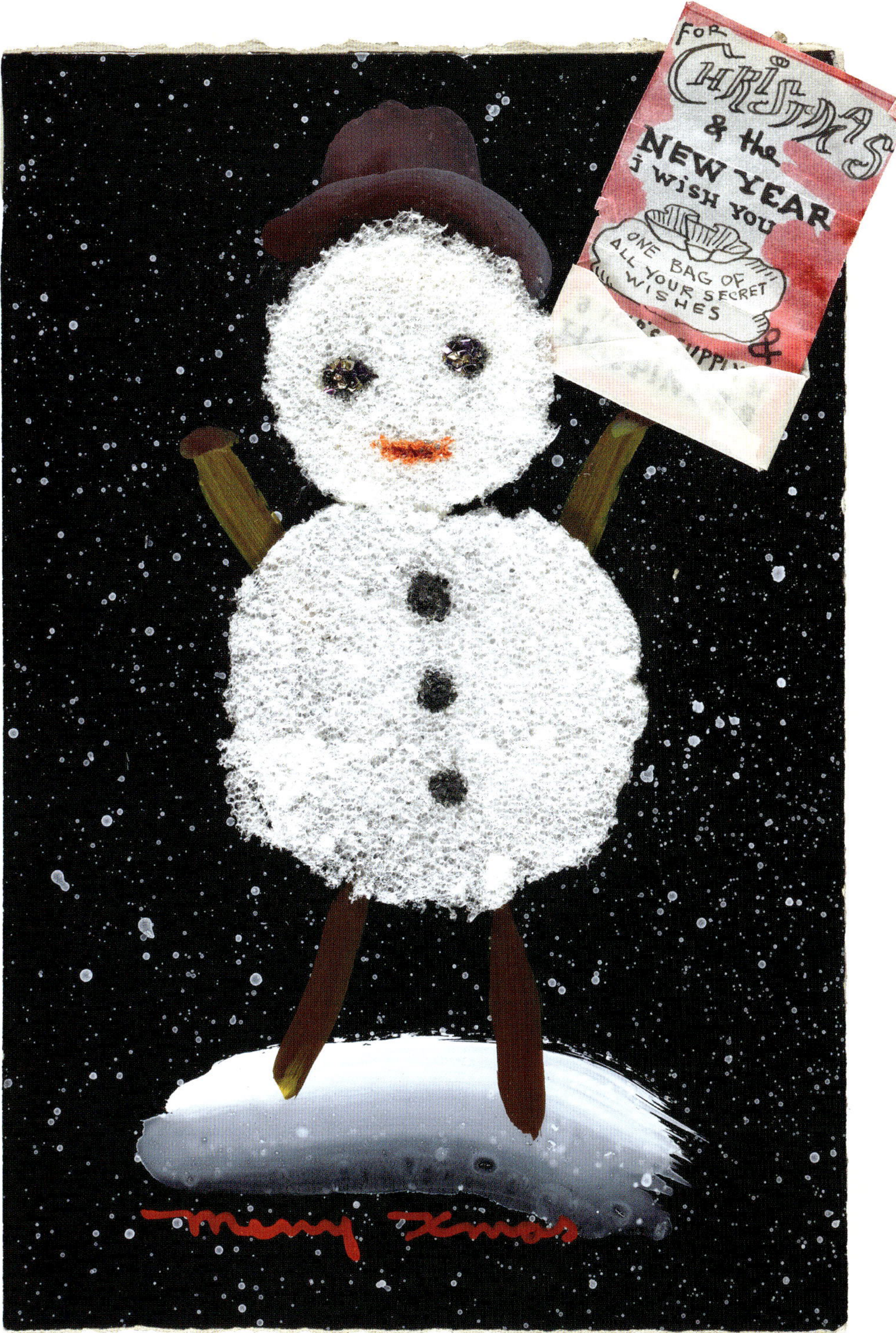
FOR CHRISTMAS & the NEW YEAR I WISH YOU
ONE BAG OF ALL YOUR SECRET WISHES
&
Merry Xmas

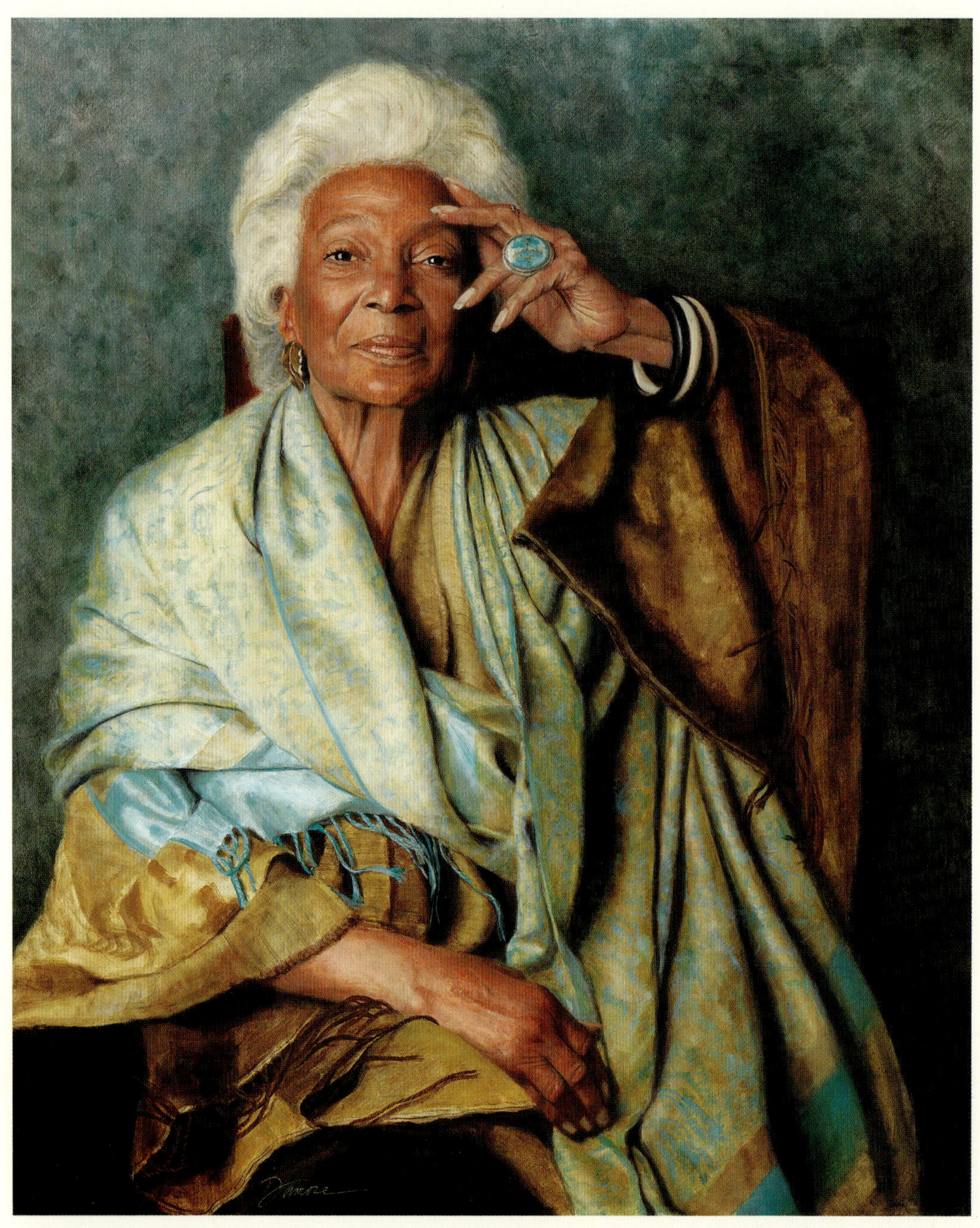

DECEMBER · JANUARY

Robin Damore (b. 1955)
Live Long and Prosper, Nichelle Nichols, Star Trek's Lieutenant Uhura at 84, 2017
Oil on canvas
46 × 40 in. (117 × 101.5 cm)
National Portrait Gallery

During the late 1960s Nichelle Nichols (1932–2022) broke new ground as Lieutenant Uhura in the television series *Star Trek*. In this portrait, she subtly mimics the "Vulcan salute" popularized by the show. From 1977 to 2015 Nichols led a successful campaign to expand recruitment for NASA's Space Shuttle astronaut corps.

KWANZAA BEGINS · BOXING DAY (CAN.)

SUNDAY
26

●

MONDAY
27

TUESDAY
28

WEDNESDAY
29

THURSDAY
30

NEW YEAR'S EVE

FRIDAY
31

NEW YEAR'S DAY · KWANZAA ENDS

HANUKKAH ENDS (SUNDOWN)

SATURDAY
1

DECEMBER

S	M	T	W	T	F	S
			1	2	3	4
5	6	7	8	9	10	11
12	13	14	15	16	17	18
19	20	21	22	23	24	25
26	27	28	29	30	31	

JANUARY 2028

S	M	T	W	T	F	S
						1
2	3	4	5	6	7	8
9	10	11	12	13	14	15
16	17	18	19	20	21	22
23	24	25	26	27	28	29
30	31					

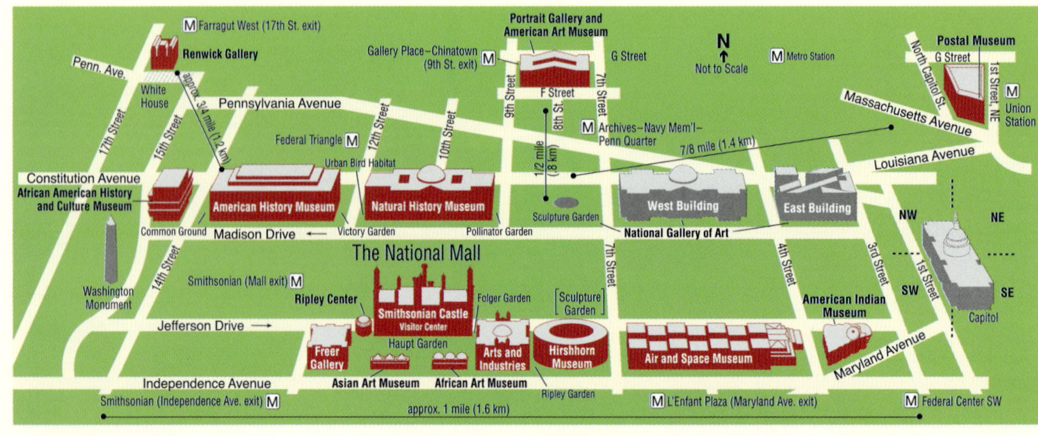

Also in Washington, DC, and Virginia:

Anacostia Community Museum, 1901 Fort Place SE

National Zoological Park, 3001 Connecticut Avenue NW

National Air and Space Museum, Steven F. Udvar-Hazy Center
14390 Air and Space Museum Parkway, Chantilly, Virginia

In New York City:

Cooper Hewitt, Smithsonian Design Museum, 2 East 91st Street and Fifth Avenue

National Museum of the American Indian, George Gustav Heye Center, One Bowling Green

America's Museum—with Global Reach

The Smithsonian Institution is the world's largest museum, education, and research complex. Founded in 1846 through the bequest of Englishman James Smithson (1765–1829), the Smithsonian continues to inspire the present and shape the future by preserving our cultural heritage, discovering new knowledge, and sharing its vast resources with the world.

Visiting the Smithsonian

You may plan your visit via the Smithsonian's website, www.si.edu, or by calling Smithsonian Information at (202) 633-1000 on Monday–Friday, 9 A.M.–5 P.M. For National Zoo information, call (202) 633-4480.

When you arrive in Washington, DC, we encourage you to begin your visit at the Smithsonian's Information Center in the Castle, where you can find maps and brochures in several languages and speak with informed volunteer specialists.

Smithsonian museums in Washington, DC, are open daily, except on December 25. Admission to the Smithsonian museums, the National Zoo in Washington, DC, and the National Museum of the American Indian in New York City is free. The admission fee at Cooper Hewitt, Smithsonian Design Museum is waived for Friends of the Smithsonian. A parking fee is required at the Steven F. Udvar-Hazy Center and at the National Zoo. Refer to the map above for the locations of Smithsonian museums on and near the National Mall in Washington, DC.

For more information on visiting specific museums or centers—and descriptions of programs and exhibitions—please visit the websites listed on the following pages.

We look forward to hosting you.

Smithsonian Museums and Galleries on the National Mall, Washington, DC

Arts and Industries Building
900 Jefferson Drive SW (next to the Castle)
aib.si.edu

The Arts and Industries Building, completed in 1881, housed our country's first national museum. After an extensive renovation, it reopened in 2015 for special events. The Mary Livingston Ripley Garden and a vintage, operational carousel are located nearby.

Hirshhorn Museum and Sculpture Garden
Independence Avenue and 7th Street SW
hirshhorn.si.edu

The Hirshhorn Museum and Sculpture Garden is a leading voice for contemporary art and culture and provides a dynamic platform for the artists, art, and ideas of our time. The collection originated with a bequest from Joseph H. Hirshhorn (1899–1981) and now numbers more than 12,000 artworks. As one of the most visited modern art museums in the nation, the Hirshhorn activates its mission, "Come as you are, leave transformed," both in person and digitally with a robust series of performances and programs.

National Air and Space Museum
Jefferson Drive between 4th and 7th Streets SW
airandspace.si.edu

The National Air and Space Museum, one of the world's most visited museums, maintains the largest collection of historic aviation and space artifacts, including the original 1903 Wright Flyer, Charles Lindbergh's *Spirit of St. Louis*, and an Apollo lunar module. The Lockheed Martin IMAX Theater's films reveal the wonders of flight.

National Museum of African American History and Culture
1400 Constitution Avenue NW
nmaahc.si.edu

The National Museum of African American History and Culture is a place where all Americans can learn about the richness and diversity of the African American experience. Through historical artifacts, documents, and works of art, the museum's exhibitions tell an American story that unites us all.

National Museum of African Art
950 Independence Avenue SW
africa.si.edu

The National Museum of African Art celebrates Africa's rich culture across time and geography without regional, media, or historical favor. Through its more than 13,000 works of art, as well as the Eliot Elisofon Photographic Archives and the Warren M. Robbins Library, the museum seeks to convey the profound historical and contemporary connections Africa has to the rest of the world.

National Museum of American History
12th Street and Constitution Avenue NW
americanhistory.si.edu

The National Museum of American History seeks to be the most accessible, inclusive, and relevant national history museum. The home of the Star-Spangled Banner and the Revolutionary-era gunboat *Philadelphia*, the museum collects and cares for national treasures including Thomas Jefferson's lapdesk, First Ladies' gowns, Dorothy's Ruby Slippers, Prince's guitar, Alfred Rascon's Medal of Honor, and other artifacts from America's history.

National Museum of Asian Art
1050 Independence Avenue SW
asia.si.edu

The National Museum of Asian Art opened its doors to the public in 1923 as the United States' first national museum of art. It is home to more than 45,000 objects dating from the Neolithic period to today and originating from the ancient Near East to China, Japan, Korea, South and Southeast Asia, and the Islamic world. The museum holds a significant group of American works of art largely dating to the late nineteenth century. It also houses the world's largest collection of diverse works by James McNeill Whistler, including the famed Peacock Room, collected by the museum's founder, Charles Lang Freer (1854–1919).

National Museum of Natural History
10th Street and Constitution Avenue NW
naturalhistory.si.edu

The National Museum of Natural History connects people everywhere with Earth's unfolding story. The museum's collection contains more than 148 million specimens, including iconic objects like the Hope Diamond, an African bush elephant, and the Nation's *T. rex*. The museum welcomes more than 4 million visitors each year, sparking curiosity and illuminating the beauty and wonder of the natural world.

National Museum of the American Indian
4th Street and Independence Avenue SW
americanindian.si.edu

The National Museum of the American Indian is dedicated to the preservation and presentation of the diverse arts, history, and material culture of Indigenous peoples of the Western Hemisphere, from the Arctic Circle to Tierra del Fuego. The museum consists of three facilities: the museums on the National Mall and in New York City and the Cultural Resources Center in Suitland, Maryland (open by appointment).

Smithsonian Gardens
gardens.si.edu

The stunning gardens throughout the Smithsonian campus along the National Mall have all been designed to complement the adjacent museums and to enhance visitors' overall learning, appreciation, and enjoyment. The Smithsonian Gardens are open year-round, seven days a week, with the gated Enid A. Haupt Garden behind the Smithsonian Castle open from dawn to dusk.

Smithsonian Institution Building (The Castle)
1000 Jefferson Drive SW
si.edu/museums/smithsonian-institution-building

Popularly known as "the Castle," this building houses the Smithsonian's main offices and the Smithsonian Information Center, where visitors may speak with volunteer information specialists to obtain additional details and directions for museums and the National Zoo.

Smithsonian Museums and Galleries beyond the National Mall in Washington, DC, and Virginia

Anacostia Community Museum
1901 Fort Place SE
anacostia.si.edu

An empowered community controls its destiny. This idea motivates the activities of the Smithsonian's Anacostia Community Museum and drives its mission to illuminate and amplify the community's collective power. The museum serves as a catalyst for critical thought about current issues, convening community stakeholders around shared challenges, common ideals, and collective action.

Lawrence A. Fleischman Gallery of the Archives of American Art
8th and F Streets NW
aaa.si.edu

The Lawrence A. Fleischman Gallery exhibits highlights from the Archives' collection of more than 20 million primary source records, which document two centuries of our nation's artists and art communities.

National Air and Space Museum Steven F. Udvar-Hazy Center
14390 Air and Space Museum Parkway, Chantilly, VA
airandspace.si.edu/udvar-hazy-center

Near Washington Dulles International Airport, the Steven F. Udvar-Hazy Center displays more than 3,000 artifacts, including nearly 200 aircraft. Highlights include a Lockheed SR-71 Blackbird, the Boeing B-29 Superfortress *Enola Gay*, and the Space Shuttle *Discovery*.

National Portrait Gallery
8th and G Streets NW
npg.si.edu

The National Portrait Gallery's more than 26,000 paintings, prints, photographs, drawings, sculptures, and works in new media honor the individuals who have contributed to the history and culture of the United States—and the artists who have portrayed them.

National Postal Museum
2 Massachusetts Avenue NE, next to Union Station
postalmuseum.si.edu

Visitors can experience sorting and delivering the mail and design their own postage stamp at the National Postal Museum, where nearly 6 million objects and numerous interactive activities present philatelic history, celebrate letter writing, and document the mail-delivery process.

National Zoological Park
3001 Connecticut Avenue NW
nationalzoo.si.edu

The Smithsonian's National Zoo and Conservation Biology Institute inspires commitment to conservation through engaging experiences with animals and the people working to save them. Founded in 1889, the zoo is home to more than 2,200 animals across 400 species, including Asian elephants, Cuban crocodiles, and Panamanian golden frogs.

Renwick Gallery
Smithsonian American Art Museum
Pennsylvania Avenue and 17th Street NW
americanart.si.edu/visit/renwick

The Renwick Gallery is home to the Smithsonian American Art Museum's collection of contemporary craft and decorative art—one of the finest and most extensive collections of its kind. The museum's home is a National Historic Landmark, the first building built expressly as an art museum in the United States.

Smithsonian American Art Museum
8th and F Streets NW
americanart.si.edu

The Smithsonian American Art Museum, the nation's first collection of American art, is home to one of the largest and most inclusive collections of American art in the world. Spanning four centuries, its collections reveal keys aspects of America's rich artistic and cultural history and capture the aspirations, character, and imagination of the American people.

Smithsonian Museums and Galleries in New York City

Cooper Hewitt, Smithsonian Design Museum
2 East 91st Street and Fifth Avenue
cooperhewitt.org

Cooper Hewitt, Smithsonian Design Museum is steward of one of the world's most diverse and comprehensive design collections—over 215,000 objects spanning thirty centuries. Housed in the landmark Carnegie Mansion, Cooper Hewitt welcomes everyone to discover the importance of design and its power to change the world.

National Museum of the American Indian
One Bowling Green
americanindian.si.edu/visit/newyork

Nearly 1 million objects collected by George Gustav Heye (1874–1957) form the heart of the collection and represent the cultures of Indigenous peoples of the Western Hemisphere. Housed in the Alexander Hamilton US Custom House, the museum offers exhibitions, public programs, performances, and symposia.

Under Development

In 2020, Congress authorized the establishment of two new museums in Washington, DC. Planning is underway for both museums, and it may take more than a decade before they open to the public. Information about pre-opening exhibits, public programs, and additional online content can be found at the websites listed below.

National Museum of the American Latino
latino.si.edu/museum

The National Museum of the American Latino will display the rich history of Latino communities in America and showcase Latino contributions to American history, art, culture, and science.

Smithsonian American Women's History Museum
womenshistory.si.edu

The Smithsonian American Women's History Museum will amplify the stories of American women to acknowledge and empower a diversity of women's voices and recognize women's accomplishments, the history they made, and the communities they represent.

Smithsonian Research and Education

Listed below are Smithsonian units and programs that pursue research and expand knowledge in the sciences, interpret and celebrate American and worldwide culture and traditions, and develop innovative educational programs and ways to deliver information to audiences near and far. Some of these programs present temporary exhibitions open to the public in Washington and across our national Affiliate Museums.

Smithsonian Research Centers

Archives of American Art
Washington, DC
aaa.si.edu

The Archives is the world's largest resource for the study of American art, with more than 6,500 manuscript collections and 2,600 oral histories ranging from the 18th century to the present, with more than 450 collections fully digitized online.

Center for Astrophysics Harvard & Smithsonian
Cambridge, MA
cfa.harvard.edu/sao

The Center for Astrophysics Harvard & Smithsonian (CfA), which includes the Smithsonian Astrophysical Observatory, is one of the largest astrophysics institutions in the world. The CfA develops and operates ground-based telescopes and space telescopes including the NASA Chandra X-ray Observatory, the NASA TEMPO satellite, and the SWEAP instrument on the Parker Solar Probe.

Center for Folklife and Cultural Heritage
Washington, DC
folklife.si.edu

Through the Smithsonian Folklife Festival, Smithsonian Folkways Recordings, Ralph Rinzler Folklife Archives, and education initiatives, the center connects communities across cultures—cultivating curiosity, understanding, and belonging for all people.

Museum Conservation Institute
Suitland, MD
si.edu/mci

State-of-the-art analytical techniques are used to study the provenance, composition, and cultural context of artistic, anthropological, and historical objects.

Smithsonian Conservation Biology Institute
Front Royal, VA
nationalzoo.si.edu/conservation

In partnership with the National Zoo, the institute's scientists are leaders in the study, protection, and restoration of threatened species, habitats, and ecosystems.

Smithsonian Environmental Research Center
Edgewater, MD
serc.si.edu

This is the world's leading research center for environmental studies of the coastal zone, and its research spans global change and the effects of chemicals on our landscape.

Smithsonian Libraries and Archives
Washington, DC
librariesarchives.si.edu

The Smithsonian Libraries and Archives is a system of 21 library branches and an institutional archive. It maintains a collection of almost 3 million library volumes and 44,000 cubic feet of archival materials. The Libraries and Archives serves as an educational resource for the Smithsonian Institution, the global research community, and the public.

Smithsonian Marine Station
Fort Pierce, FL
sms.si.edu

The station specializes in studies of Florida's marine biodiversity and ecosystems.

Smithsonian Tropical Research Institute
Republic of Panama
stri.si.edu

The institute studies tropical biodiversity and its importance to human welfare, trains students to conduct research in the area, and promotes conservation by increasing public awareness of tropical ecosystems.

Smithsonian Education and Access

Office of Fellowships and Internships
si.edu/ofi

Smithsonian staff guide the independent research of graduate students and doctoral candidates.

Smithsonian Affiliations
affiliations.si.edu

This national outreach program establishes long-term museum partnerships to share collections and resources.

Smithsonian Asian Pacific American Center
apa.si.edu

The center is committed to documenting, celebrating, and sharing the rich and diverse art, history, and culture of Asian American, Native Hawaiian, and Pacific Islander peoples and communities.

Smithsonian Associates
smithsonianassociates.org

The nation's largest museum-based education program annually presents 750 tours, performances, and seminars.

Smithsonian Center for Learning and Digital Access
learninglab.si.edu/about

The center creates models and methods to empower learners to bring ideas to life through Smithsonian resources.

Smithsonian Institution Traveling Exhibition Service
sites.si.edu

This service creates exhibitions that bring knowledge, discovery, and experiences to people across America and beyond.

Smithsonian Science Education Center
ssec.si.edu

The center transforms the teaching and learning of K–12 science in American classrooms and beyond.

Smithsonian Enterprises

Smithsonian Enterprises generates income in support of the Smithsonian's mission. Learn more about Smithsonian Enterprises at smithsonian.com.

Smithsonian Retail includes the museum retail stores, IMAX theaters, licensed commercial products, Smithsonian Books trade publishing, the e-commerce website smithsonianstore.com and the Smithsonian direct mail-order catalog, restaurants, and other visitor concessions.

Smithsonian Media include *Smithsonian* magazine and online web services and the Smithsonian TV Channel and Digital Studio.

Smithsonian Travel is made up of Smithsonian Journeys adult educational travel and Smithsonian Student Travel.

Notes

Notes

Notes

Notes

Notes

Notes

Notes

Notes

Notes